"*Herbert Lui is a gifted writer, an or thinker. He always has something i generous.*"

— Rob Walker, journalist and author of *The Art of Noticing*

"*Having done nearly 10,000 drawings up to this point, there's no secret to art except consistent, creative doing. It's not easy, but once you embrace 'Process' over 'Result' you'll find you have a lifetime of learning and discovery and creative freedom ahead of you. If you want to learn this method and philosophy, this book is a great place to start.*"

— Shantell Martin, visual artist

"*We're all creative beings, but sometimes we need a bit of help. Herbert offers a brilliant toolkit of 75 prompts and ideas you can apply right away to do your best work. I'm a big believer in small steps that lead to massive results, but if you're in a tough spot it can be hard to figure out exactly what those steps are. Creative Doing is the perfect guide when you feel blocked or when looking for inspiration to take things to the next level.*"

— Rick Pastoor, co-founder of Rise and author of *GRIP*

"*Choose your passion, then choose a time each day, and dedicate it to only pursuing this passion. For me it was painting, and I decided to do it every day, at lunchtime. I wish I had had this book to guide me when I got started, but luckily, you have Herbert Lui's insight into the creative mind as a roadmap in starting your journey.*"

— Michael "Big Mike" Saviello, visual artist

Other Books Available at Holloway.com

Art for Money: Up Your Freelance Game and Get Paid What You're Worth
Michael Ardelean
Learn to apply simple and practical principles to get organized, grow your business, and stay true to your art. The missing manual for every creative freelancer.

Stop Asking Questions: How to Lead High-Impact Interviews and Learn Anything from Anyone
Andrew Warner
Master the craft of interviewing with this complete digital package. A veteran podcast host of 2000+ episodes reveals the secrets of deeper conversation. Includes exclusive audio and video resources for podcasters, salespeople, entrepreneurs, and anyone who knows the value of learning.

Land Your Dream Design Job
Dan Shilov
A guide for product designers, from portfolio to interview to job offer.

The Holloway Guide to Equity Compensation
Joshua Levy, Joe Wallin et al.
Stock options, RSUs, job offers, and taxes—a detailed reference, explained from the ground up.

The Holloway Guide to Remote Work
Katie Womersley, Juan Pablo Buriticá et al.
A comprehensive guide to building, managing, and adapting to working with distributed teams.

Ask Me This Instead: Flip the Interview to Land Your Dream Job
Kendra Haberkorn
This guide is your companion as you take control of the interviewing process and find the job that's right for you.

Founding Sales: The Early-Stage Go-To-Market Handbook
Pete Kazanjy
This tactical handbook distills early sales first principles, and teaches the skills required for going from being a founder to early salesperson, and eventually becoming an early sales leader.

Creative Doing

Creative Doing

75 PRACTICAL EXERCISES TO UNBLOCK YOUR CREATIVE POTENTIAL IN YOUR WORK, HOBBY, OR NEXT CAREER

Herbert Lui

Whether creative work is part of your full-time job or personal passion, a few simple and powerful tools can unlock a unique creative process that works for you.

RACHEL JEPSEN, EDITOR
BERNICE LIU, ILLUSTRATOR

HOLLOWAY

Published in the United States by Holloway, San Francisco
Holloway.com

Cover and illustrations by Bernice Liu
Cover design by Order (New York) and Andy Sparks
Interior design by Joshua Levy and Jennifer Durrant
Production by Nathaniel Hemminger
Print engineering by Titus Wormer

Typefaces: Tiempos Text and National 2
by Kris Sowersby of Klim Type Foundry

Print version 1.0
doc 8bad05 · pipeline 1bc509 · genbook 91a734 · 2022-05-13

Want More Out of This Book?

Holloway publishes books online. As a reader of this special full-access print edition, you are granted personal access to the paid digital edition, which you can read and share on the web, and offers commentary, updates, and corrections.

Claim your account by visiting: **holloway.com/print20428**

If you wish to recommend the book to others, suggest they visit **holloway.com/cd** to learn more and purchase their own digital or print copy.

The author welcomes your feedback! Please consider adding comments or suggestions to the book online so others can benefit. Or say hello@holloway.com. Thank you for reading.

The Holloway team

TABLE OF CONTENTS

INTRODUCTION

1 Purpose from Process

Like many people aspiring to do creative work, I wasn't born into a family of artists, or into unearned income that would enable me to pursue my art full-time. I didn't participate in any talent shows, I've dealt with years of underestimating myself, and I wasn't taught how to be creative in school. I wrote, and rewrote, this book not because I'm a creative genius revealing a secret, but because it was the book I needed to read.

I have been obsessed with the mystery of the creative process for over a decade. Successful artists had figured out how to do great creative work. Why couldn't I?

I sought out every chance to find an answer. In the first half of the 2010s, I pored through academic literature, biographies, and memoirs. I interviewed prominent recording artists and authors on their processes. I seized every opportunity I could to ask people about their creative processes and for detailed examples of what they did to make their work. I immersed myself in a study of each individual's creative process itself—the observable parts of ideation, creation, and release.

Creative work sounds simple enough ("Just make stuff!"), but it can feel painful when you don't know how to make sense of it. For many years, I experienced a version of the creative block that might sound familiar: numbness. I wrote at a media company, started an editorial studio,[1] and supported other people's creative projects with marketing. I felt I had to suppress my true creative urges in order to make money. I tried my best to make it work.

Because I had so little time for the creative work I wanted to do—to write and express my own ideas—I became completely attached to the results I could attain. I wasn't practicing, I was pushing. After months and years of this struggle, I realized that I was missing a piece of the puzzle: my own creative purpose.

---

1. https://wondershuttle.com/

Finding my creative purpose involved letting go of every impulse and habit that made me successful at my work projects, and shifting my focus away from results into the process. Process is about consistently making time and energy to practice every day, rather than intensely pursuing a creative project and then burning out, falling out of love with it, and becoming resentful. It's about creating a lot of work that meets a standard I set for myself. There's a chance you probably feel the same way I did; that throughout each day, the thought comes to you, "I'm meant to do something, and it's not what's in front of me right now." What does it mean when you find yourself creatively blocked? What if that wave of inspiration never comes, and how are you supposed to know how long to wait? What if you can't get started, or begin but don't finish, or are always too busy with everything else?

2 What's In This Book

Great ideas aren't found, they're made, through consistent creative practice. Creative thinking comes from creative doing.

Influential painter Chuck Close said in an interview for *Inside the Painter's Studio*:

> *Inspiration is for amateurs—the rest of us just show up and get to work. And the belief that things will grow out of the activity itself and that you will—through work—bump into other possibilities and kick open other doors that you would never have dreamt of if you were just sitting around looking for a great "art idea."*

Or, as Picasso said, "Inspiration exists, but it has to find you working."[2]

What you're reading is the book I wish I had at the beginning of my journey, one with prompts that would encourage, stimulate, and strengthen the creative process.

---

2. https://libquotes.com/pablo-picasso/quote/lbx5g7f

My approach to creativity is to bring together the hands, head, and heart, by focusing on quantity (doing as much as you can), quality (improving your abilities and honing your taste and style), and purpose (knowing what you are creating for).

This book provides exercises to move each of these levers forward.

A lot has happened since I wrote and independently published this work—I got a chance to work with a publisher (Holloway) to expand and revise the book. It has made a difference with some readers, and my writing has reached millions of viewers. Regardless of these external rewards, the thing I'm most proud of is that I found a way to make my creative process work throughout the other commitments of my life—work, relationship, family, friends, and health.

The incredible intrinsic and extrinsic rewards of the creative process do not mean that it comes easily. Whether you're choosing to make a vocation out of your creativity, you're seeking a new hobby, or you're simply figuring out how to make time for your creativity, this book will enable you to find the process that works for you. It's something that nobody else can teach you, that only you can learn for yourself.

3 Who This Book Is For

If you're reading this, I'm sure you're a fan of an artist, a field, or a subculture, eager to make your contribution through remixing, interpreting, or creating something.

You could be starting your journey to creating and publishing your work online. You might be working a full-time job in a field unrelated to your creativity, and recently left or are considering leaving. Maybe you want to try a creative hobby outside of your day job.

Maybe you just know that you've got something to give to the world that you don't have a chance to express right now.

Michael Saviello, a manager at Astor Place Hairstylists, was inspired to pick up his paintbrush after he saw his friend and customer Rafael Hines self-publish his book *Bishop's War* by writing from midnight to 3 a.m., sleeping until 6 a.m., and going to his full-time job. He resolved to paint during his lunch hour; several months into this habit, he debuted at his local art gallery. He said in an interview with Humans of New York,[3] "My entire life, I'd been saying, 'I can do that.' I always knew it. But I finally did it. So now other people know it too."

In this book, you'll hear firsthand from Saviello, as well as other acclaimed creatives like Shantell Martin and DJ Dahi, to get a better sense of how they do what they do. That's the promise of *Creative Doing*. Whether it's dull or torturously painful, you are experiencing a block on your creativity, and this book will enable you to unblock it, express it, and get it flowing again.

You'll find this book useful if you are:

- A content creator online, who wants to rediscover the joy of creativity and connection, find new sources of inspiration, refine your creative process, and deepen your craft.
- A creative independent who wants to restore your passion, rediscover a creative outlet that isn't commercially driven, and to work through creative blocks.
- A creative hobbyist who wants to figure out your creative purpose, pursue creative excellence, and make time for your creative endeavors.
- An in-house creative who wants to be more creative at work, by finding new ways to solve professional problems and apply your creative skills, developing new technical skills, and getting more comfortable with brainstorming and ideation.

You may find that more than one of these roles describe your situation. Making progress with your creative work will require you to commit essential amounts of time, at least three to five hours per week, in researching, learning, or trying to participate in a form of creativity or art. Maybe you're already along on your journey, and are spending money each month seeking inspiration, or maintaining your software or equipment for your practice. You're clearly interested in creative expression, and you're now encountering some of the other challenges that come along the road—uncertainty in the quality of your work, developing your skills, finding your creative purpose.

I wrote this book to honor and support you, the emerging, competitive, and practicing creators and artists dedicated to exploring your creative potential.

---

3. https://www.facebook.com/humansofnewyork/posts/6093664437374272

4 How to Use the Prompts

Nine polyhedral shapes adorn the cover of this book. Mathematically speaking, there are an infinite number of possible polyhedral shapes—just as there are an infinite number of versions and variations of each piece of work in the creative process. Each new day creates an opportunity to make a new shape. It's through making a lot of shapes that the ones you like start to emerge.

Each of this book's 75 prompts will suggest an action, propose a new way of thinking about what's in front of you, or tell you a story. It's through this action, and ensuing ideas that your brain generates, that will allow new breakthroughs and insights to reach you.

The prompts are organized in nine chapters, each with a path that you can follow.

I'd recommend starting with Part I: Start the Creative Process, which will help you begin a new creative endeavor with the right mindset. You'll put together your starting points—places where your work can develop from—and learn to let go of the expectations and outcomes you'd had in mind to open up to something even better. You'll also learn how the creative process works through hands-on experience.

Part II: From Action Comes Progress, is all about, well, action—first, producing as much creative work as possible, then defining and practicing quality work, sharing your work, and soliciting and integrating feedback.

The prompts in Part III: Creative Purpose, will help you slow down and get back to basics, trust yourself, and have clarity of vision.

That said, these prompts can also be approached any other way. Jumping to a prompt you think will speak to where you are right now is a great idea. Prompts also reference and link to other prompts—you're encouraged to choose your own adventure. Overall, and in any order, this book will encourage you to work within the many constraints that life presents, get other people involved with your work, improve your craft, experiment with new ideas and methods, and build a life rich through creativity, whether or not you choose to make it your full-time profession.

Here are some other starting points:

- **How can I break through my creative block?**

  - Relinquish Results$^{\S6.8}$
  - Set a 10-day Quota$^{\S7.5}$

PART I: START THE CREATIVE PROCESS

"I've been making music for a long time. I've learned a lot of stuff along the way, but I don't let that get in the way. I don't let that impede the process of making something new."

— Rick Rubin

In *Orbiting the Giant Hairball*, Gordon MacKenzie, who led creative for three decades at Hallmark Cards, paints the portrait of "a rotund gentleman in a $700, power-blue, pinstripe suit," leaning on the fence and watching cows eat grass. He yells, "You slackers get to work, or I'll have you butchered!"

MacKenzie likens this person's ignorance about milking cows to common feelings about the creative process.[4] He knows that cows eat grass and produce milk but has no idea what happens in between—he wants measurable evidence of creativity without honoring the invisible creative activity it takes to produce that. You might know someone who bears resemblance to the gentleman. Perhaps it's you.

In July 2013 I published a blog post titled, "Why Quantity Should Be Your Priority."[5] I proposed that quantity could be a reliable tool to improve quality. The response was immediate. Musicians, writers, designers, CEOs, investors, and even professional gamers virtually nodded in agreement that repetition and purposeful development of the skill were the only way to become a master of the craft. As I write this, the article has been read over 200,000 times, shared thousands of times, and even added to a university's coursework.

This fascination with the quantity, quality, and the creative process, would take me on a journey into the lives of prominent artists of the past, and to conversations with contemporary artists of today. Nearly a decade after originally publishing the article, and through this decade-

---

4. https://herbertlui.net/four-step-creative-process/

5. https://herbertlui.medium.com/why-quantity-should-be-your-priority-3bc2b16fe3f5

long research process, I understand that it resonated because it laid bare a truth we already fundamentally know: creativity doesn't just take place inside our brains; it's a full body experience. And as much value as we place on the finished product as evidence of our creativity, we need to value creative *doing*. You can't get the milk without standing around eating grass.

In Part I, we're going to explore prompts designed to help you pick the creative operation and process best suited for you, to set the environment that enables your creativity to flow, and to allow yourself to start fun, even occasionally profound, creative projects.

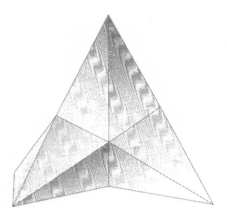

5 Set Up Starting Points

> "*My observation is that the doers are the major thinkers. The people that really create the things that change this industry are both the thinker and doer in one person.*"
>
> — Steve Jobs[6]

You probably think about doing more creative work a lot. At a certain point, it's time to just pick up the brush and start painting. "Many people die with their music still in them," physicist, poet, and polymath Oliver Wendell Holmes Sr. said. "Too often it is because they are always getting ready to live. Before they know it, time runs out."

There is no *right* way to do creative work; the only wrong way is not to do anything. This chapter will help you get started.

---

6. Interview with Steve Jobs, 1990.[7] "The Paperback Computer," *The Machine That Changed The World*. Episode 3, New Television Workshop, 1992.

7. https://openvault.wgbh.org/catalog/V_AD9E0BC353BF435E83F28DEF165D4F40

5.1 *Choose a Creative Operation*

Whether you have grand ambitions or are simply curious to explore, it helps to begin concretely. Pick a creative operation you will explore.

If you don't have a creative area to work in and are nervous about getting started, think about what area might expand on your existing skills. If your job involves writing, for example, and you enjoy doing that, creative writing might be an interesting place for you to start.

If you already do creative work but feel blocked, consider a new creative operation—it could be something entirely different than your usual work. This decision could be a temporary experiment, and not necessarily the medium you're going to stick with forever.[8]

You could start with a community you appreciate. For example, if you regularly read a subreddit like r/startups,[9] you could start by responding to questions or sharing business opportunities you've noticed.

Look into your routines and the daily things you enjoy, and list all of the possible related creative fields. If you find yourself hanging out at jazz clubs, you might want to try something related to the recording arts or mixology. If you really appreciate hip-hop, you might want to try songwriting, spoken word poetry, making instrumental tracks, stage design, or designing streetwear. Many of your interests contain or are connected with a host of creative possibilities that you can try.

You might be saying, "Jazz club? I work 80 hours a week." If you haven't made creative work a part of your life in the past and don't know where to begin, start by taking yourself out on "artist dates," as *The Artist's Way* author Julia Cameron suggests. Visit a museum by yourself, letting your feet carry you to the work that draws you in. Go to a concert and sit as close to the stage as you can—which instrument do you find yourself hearing the loudest, which musician do you watch while the band plays? Spend three hours on Saturday reading a book outside of the genre you normally read. You may find that a clear answer emerges from expanding your horizons.

---

8. I appreciate that it's not always so simple to commit to a creative operation—especially if that feels like giving up other passions and curiosities. While you're picking one now, it certainly doesn't mean you can't try others. If you find yourself blocked and struggling to choose, check out *Refuse to Choose!* by Barbara Sher.

9. https://www.reddit.com/r/startups/

Lastly, consider the objects that you love.[10] If you've always loved light fixtures, you can choose an operation related to industrial design. If you like skillets, kitchen knives, and cookbooks, you can try an operation related to the culinary arts. (See Select One Tool.[§7.1])

Michael Saviello, also known as Big Mike, paints during his lunch hour inside Astor Place Hairstylists, where he has been a manager for 30 years. It's not difficult for Big Mike to paint during the lunch hour at his day job. "This is my favorite part of the day," he says. If you find yourself paralyzed by choosing one creative operation—which can be difficult!—then stick with what feels good to you. Ask yourself, "Could *this* be the favorite part of my day?"

Once you've narrowed in on a creative operation, getting started might feel like another task in your to-do list—even a chore, on some days. Instead of feeling "I *need* to do this," you can cultivate the attitude of "I *get* to do this." If you don't enjoy it, then you need to ask yourself what you're doing and why. Is the goal something different from enjoyment, or passion? Are you driven to change your career path, or to learn a new skill for a different reason?

Questions like this might enable you to realize whether the operation you've picked is really the right one for you. Lindsay Jean Thomson's first 100 day project[§7.5] was taking a photo each day, only for her to realize that writing suited her better. Nonetheless, Jean Thomson fulfilled her 100 days of photography. Some days must have been hard and others easy; but she made it happen.

Be easy with yourself—if you don't actually like it, don't force it. It may help to remind yourself that you're practicing this skill in service of what you really like. (For example, you need to practice research in order to become a good writer.)

You may also realize that, after a few days of practice, it really becomes the best (or second best, or third best) part of some of your days. This isn't necessarily meant to be a lasting, permanent, "I've found *the thing!*" but rather, "I've found *something*."

Many people pick up two or three different crafts throughout their lives. Maybe you've found the first one, and the second one awaits you somewhere down the line. Once you've found it and committed to your chosen creative operation, the next moves are to figure out how to fit it

---

10. https://herbertlui.net/how-to-find-your-passion-with-objects/

into your day, and how to make sure you keep doing it. You can liken this to the experimental process of a scientist: when you choose an operation, you're coming up with hypotheses of what you may or may not like. When you observe something doesn't work, you've completed the experiment, and are free to test another hypothesis.

5.2 *Work with What You Have*

Artist Chuck Close describes the tendency for artists to spend years finding, designing, and outfitting the perfect space to work. Once the space is done, though, they end up selling it and building another. Close says in *Inside the Painter's Studio*, "It seems more often than not a way to keep from having to work. But I could paint anywhere. I made big paintings in the tiniest bedrooms, garages, you name it. You know, once I have my back to the room, I could be anywhere. I could care less."

Even before we start our creative work, it's easy to find reasons to stop—it's common to say, "I can't create because I don't have professional tools or the right space." We spend hours—maybe even days—getting around obstacles that we set up for ourselves. Even for something like writing, which can involve as little as a single tool, you can stop yourself from actually working by cycling through an endless series of questions: what word processing software or notebook should I use? Where should I publish my work? If I'm deciding to set up my own blog, which software should I use? Should I be building my audience first instead of writing?

These questions are all well and good. They also have absolutely nothing to do with writing. Just put the pen on a page (or even a scrap piece of paper), and start writing.

In reality, we don't need anything except our brains and bodies to practice our creative work. The goal is to put this reality into practice with the fewest tools possible, in any environment.

↬ **Or flip this prompt:** *Find the Simplest Element of Your Craft*[§6.1]

5.3 *Adorn Your Space*

Chuck Close may be able to turn his back on any room and get to work, but shutting out the world might not work for you—or not work all the time.

You may not have a Parisian atelier with floor-to-ceiling windows (or need one) but there are ways to make the space you do have more inspiring and conducive to creative work.

In his biography of Leonardo da Vinci, Walter Isaacson quotes da Vinci describing an artist at work: "The painter sits in front of his work at perfect ease. He is well dressed and wields a very light brush dipped in delicate color. He adorns himself with the clothes he fancies; his home is clean and filled with delightful pictures, and he is often accompanied by music or by the reading of various beautiful works." (In psychology, enclothed cognition covers[11] the influence of clothes on the mind of the person wearing it.)

You can also experiment with the temperature, and be mindful of how that influences your thought process. Singer-songwriter Ester Dean says,[12] "I always have an electric heater behind my feet, but I like to be comfortable so that I can be vulnerable."

Because this is a book about creative doing—which means creativity in the physical world—test some things out that play with your senses, to see what affects your creative mind. Light a candle or apply some essential oils. Create a playlist of songs that pump you up, and then try music that calms you down. If your work is mostly done on the go and on the screen, you can also take some time to make your virtual environment—screen brightness, wallpapers, and software—more conducive to creative work. Whatever or wherever it is, make your environment a place you want to spend time every day.

5.4 *Draft, Demo, and Sketch*

No creative work emerges finished. Preliminary work is rough, and often bears little resemblance to the polished, completed product released to the public.

Mozart would often start a piece, set it aside, and then pick it back up months or years later. Musicologist Ulrich Konrad[13] called these beginnings "departure points ... a delineation of intellectual places to which

---

11. https://www.sciencedirect.com/science/article/abs/pii/S0022103112000200
12. https://www.vibe.com/music/music-news/
    view-from-the-studio-ester-dean-interview-332119/
13. https://www.newyorker.com/magazine/2006/07/24/the-storm-of-style

Mozart could return as necessary." Each field has different names to describe preliminary creative work. In writing, a preliminary work is called a "draft." In recording arts and software, preliminary work is called a "demo" and often used to demonstrate the artist's or group's capabilities and the work's possibilities. In visual art, preliminary work is called a "sketch," and used to assist in making the final work.

Preliminary work is not optional, and every version of preliminary work is crucial for improving the work we're making. This stage is far too early to demand perfection; it's best to keep expectations low,[§6.7] to refrain from self-criticism, and to support psychological safety (the feeling that it's okay to make mistakes) to allow every single detail of the idea to flow out.

One of the most fascinating properties of the creative process is, every version of a piece of work can be seen as preliminary work. While you can finish different versions and variations of a project, there doesn't have to be a final sense of completion. Pablo Picasso said, "If it were possible ... there would never be a 'finished' canvas but just different states of a single painting." And here's W. H. Auden paraphrasing a line of Paul Valéry's: "A poem is never finished, only abandoned."

Dacoury Natche and his collaborators worked on the song "Time" on Childish Gambino's *3.15.20* album for nearly two years. Natche said there are multiple versions of the song, including one that sounds more like a party, and another that sounds more like a live version. He was willing to commit that time because the song held potential. He described his mindset: "Let's just try as many versions as we can because I know this song feels like something special."

Our goal here is to practice not worrying about whether or not something is perfect. Instead, it's about creating one version of a project that will likely either be improved upon in the future or serve as inspiration for something else. The key is to cultivate the commitment and conviction to declare that something is done, for now.

"Anything you do is basically a demo until it comes out, or it's present," said Dacoury Natche. "Sometimes even if it comes out, it still can be a demo." It's fitting that Natche brings this up, since iterating on final products often takes place in music through remixes, samples, and covers.

It might sound counterintuitive, or even painful or scary, to your inner craftsperson to complete work in so little time that it doesn't feel ready. That's the whole point. Your judgment of your work may not reflect how somebody else interprets or experiences it. It's fine to know something that you made isn't your best, and still declare this version of it complete—or to release it to the world. The work that resonates with the most people may not be the one that you declare to be the best; still, it can make an impact on people.

This prompt requires that you focus on starting something and finishing a version of it. Think of everything you make as a demo, a sketch, or a draft. Remove all ideas of expectations and goals, and focus simply on the process and taking a draft to a state where you declare it finished and acceptable as a working version. With every end comes a new beginning. It's only by finishing a preliminary version of your work imperfectly, that you can start a new one.

5.5 *Organize Your Departure Points*

Every effort begins somewhere, from some idea, some element of work. The vision of this prompt is to build your own collection of elements that you can apply and combine with others, sometimes more than once.

It's important to keep these *departure points* as small as possible. These days, we are blessed with technology that can store and organize all of our departure points.

For example, even though I'd written hundreds of articles in my 20s, many of the ideas—points, stats, and quotes—embedded in them were too interlinked and dense for me to move around and re-use in new ones. My solution to that was to extract the ideas and put them into index cards and Notion[14] for my Zettelkasten note-taking system,[15] which I learned from *How to Take Smart Notes*[16] by Sönke Ahrens. Each stat would get its own separate index card.

It's possible to do this with other forms as well. If you're in the recording arts, you can separately save different elements of songs for easy access. If you're in visual arts, you can work digitally and do the same by saving elements in different layers or files altogether. Be descriptive in your filename so you know what to search later. I'd highly encourage you

---

14. https://www.notion.so/

15. https://herbertlui.net/8-lessons-from-800-note-cards-in-the-zettelkasten/

16. https://takesmartnotes.com/

to take even just a few minutes to set up a simple system for staying organized.

This can also be as simple as starting a project with a banker's box—a
literal cardboard box—and keeping everything related in there like choreographer and author Twyla Tharp does. Or it could mean setting an hour
every Monday to review your notes in your journal and phone.

Combining and connecting are key parts of any creative process. As
you go through these departure points, and your mind soaks them in,
you'll notice that new ideas and connections start to emerge.

5.6 *Say Yes*

If you go to an improv comedy class, you'll see that participants are
encouraged to agree to and build upon everybody else's ideas. Comedian,
filmmaker, writer Tina Fey calls this the "Rule of Agreement" in her memoir *Bossypants*, describing it as a reminder to:

> *"Respect what your partner has created" and to at least start
> from an open-minded place. Start with a YES and see where that
> takes you.*

So try saying *yes* to every prompt or idea from others, at least once. If
the need arises, you are free to make modifications and to add an element
of your own to the prompt. I would be extremely happy to hear that you'd
augmented one of these prompts to fit you better.

When you say yes, you train your brain to let go of your preferences and
expectations, and to let go of them to work with whatever's in front of you.

The other benefit to saying yes is that it opens your mind up to chaotic,
creative, energy. If you feel like you don't have this—like you're not creative, or you're better at executing other people's ideas, or that your work
sucks—you'll need to trust me on this for now. The energy may simply be
dormant or latent, waiting for you to tap into it.

Chaotic energy is incredibly valuable. You could consider it to be the raw material of all creative work. One of the best explanations of this comes from Professor Betty Flowers's response to her students' woes of getting started writing, which I learned from my editor on this book, Rachel Jepsen.[17] Flowers writes:

> *What happens when you get stuck is that two competing energies are locked horn to horn, pushing against each other. One is the energy of what I'll call your "madman." He is full of ideas, writes crazily and perhaps rather sloppily, gets carried away by enthusiasm or anger, and if really let loose, could turn out ten pages an hour.*
>
> *The second is a kind of critical energy—what I'll call the "judge." He's been educated and knows a sentence fragment when he sees one. He peers over your shoulder and says, "That's trash!" with such authority that the madman loses his crazy confidence and shrivels up. You know the judge is right—after all, he speaks with the voice of your most imperious English teacher. But for all his sharpness of eye, he can't create anything.*

Flowers so well articulates the innate duality of the madman and the judge that exists in all forms of creative work, between making and releasing, recording and editing, working and reworking, programming and debugging, doodling and drawing.

When each of us grows up, we learn to seek validation, approvals, and reviews for our work. We grow to depend on the critical energy from the judge, at the cost of starving the madman of the very crucial, chaotic, energy.

It's later in the book—when you're well used to agreeing with where your inner chaotic energy is taking you, that you'll reconnect with your opinions, taste, and discernment. As Rachel Jepsen writes, "In order to get to unity you have to begin with chaos."

---

17. https://every.to/the-long-conversation/first-thought-best-thought

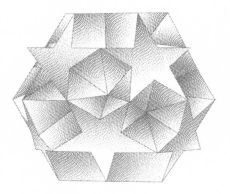

6 Make Your Work a Craft

"In writing about the sea I have learned the important truth that a writer's subject is always far bigger and more important than the writer himself."

— Rachel Carson[18]

Writing in *The Craftsman*, sociologist Richard Sennett explores how culture is made. He defines craftsmanship as, "An enduring, basic human impulse, the desire to do a job well for its own sake." A craftsperson is "dedicated to good work for its own sake. Theirs is practical activity, but their labor is not simply a means to another end."

When a person is dedicated to doing something as well as it can be done—beyond commercial and external interests—their labor becomes craft.

The craftsperson is self-reliant and imaginative; even in the endless repetition of piano scales or in the sharpening of a pencil, the craftsperson can see ways to improve their work. A craftsperson can try new materials

---

18. Popova, Maria. *Figuring*. Vintage Books, 2020, p. 504.

and apply their attention to detail and observational skills in different contexts. They work with intention at every level. They may get into a creative flow where work comes easily. But it is never mindless. Over time, the craftsperson can master the methods of a form, and then add new ones. They develop their own style and become recognizable.

Approach your work like a craftsperson. Improve your craft. Find places and people that enable you to work on your craft, and turn away from what stifles or discourages it. Set up your life so that you can work on your craft. Pick friends and partners who support you. If you feel the fire for the craft dwindling, find a new approach to it. Or, if you're interested in exploring a new kind of craft, do it. Focusing on craft usually means letting go of external judgment, like what the buyers, the markets, or the algorithms reward. Transcend the labels of commerce; be a craftsperson. In order to support this call to action, the following sections will describe the concepts that put the craft first.

6.1 *Find the Simplest Element of Your Craft*

One of Shantell Martin's most popular projects involves two objects: a black medium-width Staedtler Lumocolor marker and a white wall. Using the permanent marker, she'll cover an entire wall in elaborate line work. She also draws murals on walls and surfaces at live shows,[19] incorporating an element of performance art to her process.

Martin has said,[20] "It takes a ton of work and practice to get to the point when a line is a true reflection of yourself."

It can feel incredibly inspiring—and overwhelming—to consider a final body of work. Instead, as you're starting out, turn your focus away from the final vision of the project and toward the simplest element of it.

In Martin's form of visual art, each piece of her work is made up of lines. In all forms of writing, each article, book, or poem, is made up of words. In the recording arts, each bar and song is made up of notes.

---

19. https://www.youtube.com/watch?v=Ny1kgMXCpv4
20. https://www.matterofhand.com/shantell-martin/shantell-martin

As you start to discover these common elements, you'll realize final pieces of work are just polished combinations of them.

The simplest elements may take a day to learn but a lifetime to master.

↬ **Or flip this prompt:** *Work with What You Have*[§5.2]

6.2 *Remove Imaginary Barriers to Your Work*

After years of learning and applying rules, you might live within these constraints even when they don't actually apply to you. You'll feel like you're bumping into invisible walls. For me, a huge invisible wall was the traditional publishing system; I felt like I needed to have a book agent, write a book proposal, and build an audience, all before I could actually start to write a book. For years, I tortured myself with that idea that I needed the system's buy-in before I could write a book. This fixation on being accepted by the traditional institutions distracted me from the clear vision of what was in front of me and the valuable experiences and ideas I already had.

The reality is, as I found out years later, I could've written a book at any time. A book can be as simple as 20,000 words strung together. If I stitched together 20 articles at 1,000 words each, which I was writing every week, I could've put a book together. (In the traditional book publishing world, some books are even just 11,500 words.) This is true for you as well. As soon as you've figured out the simplest elements of your craft, you can start creating. Elsewhere in this book, you'll do exercises that involve finding new materials[§8.7] to work with—new lines, words, and sounds, for example—and more deliberately setting a mission[§13.2] and theme, which can be based on one specific element of your work.

Even before we start our creative work, it's easy to find reasons to stop. We don't have the equipment that the professionals use, we have no one following our work, and we're unsure if what we're trying to do is even "really" what we want to do. If you've let your craft get more complicated in your head—through the mystique and magic of creativity—it's time to let them go. Don't impose fictitious rules on yourself.

You might think you need all of that to get started, when in reality all of those resources and insights will come to you as you do the work.

6.3　*Make Idle Time*

> *"The most important thing I noticed today was that only in
> stillness can we recognize movement."*
>
> — Marina Abramović —

There is no universal creative process. But any creative process will involve various periods of *incubation*, or time spent not consciously thinking about the problem. You have likely experienced this phenomenon yourself when after hours at work spent agonizing over a problem, the solution pops into your head when you get home and take the dog for a walk. This is also known as The Shower Principle—ideas come to you when you're doing something else, like taking a shower, doing the dishes, or working on another problem entirely.

As it turns out, even if you're not concentrating on something or keeping busy, a different part of your brain activates and processes your thoughts. If you're interested in the neuroscience at work here, I suggest reading Alex Soojung-Kim Pang's *Rest*.

Practically speaking, we can't actually make ourselves process things or produce creatively faster. In fact, it's only when we allow our mind some peace and quiet that it can relax, and produce the ideas we so desire. But don't cover your mind in Netflix or podcasts—reject media's influence and let your brain settle down. Take a bath or long shower. Try meditating with or without an app. Go for a trail walk or bike ride. Let rest and distraction become part of your creative process.

↪ Or flip this prompt: *Do Your Work without Your Equipment*[§7.4]

6.4　*Make Time to Play*

"Without play, only Shit Happens. With play, Serendipity Happens," wrote David Weinberger in *The Cluetrain Manifesto*.[21]

"Work which remains permeated with the play attitude is art," wrote philosopher John Dewey.

The difference between work and play is largely intention. Play is intended for amusement, joy, and perhaps mastery, with the main intention being to continue to play. Work is intended for results, benefit, and

---

21. https://www.cluetrain.com/book/hyperorg.html

sustenance, with the main intention being to continue to survive or provide for yourself.

We already know how to play—to do something for its own sake, to
explore, to imagine. It's just that sometimes we go without it for so long
that we may forget. No wonder there are classes to teach us how to relearn
this valuable skill that was squished out of us. If you need ideas, go do
improvisational comedy or try a new instrument or a sport. Rent a bicycle
and go for a ride. Buy a Lego set and build. Draw a cartoon. Feed your creative practice (and well-being) by making time for play.

Even if you're doing it for work, you may find infusing your work with
the spirit of play to bring about an interesting opportunity or idea that
wasn't obvious to you at first.

6.5 *Lose Yourself*

Let go of your external expectations. Immerse yourself in the task at hand.

Bono wrote about Frank Sinatra,[22] "Fully inhabiting the moment during that tiny dot of time after you've pressed 'record' is what makes it eter-
nal. If, like Frank, you sing it like you'll never sing it again. If, like Frank,
you sing it like you never have before." This philosophy is applicable to
your craft; you can pretend like it's the last time you're doing your work,
the last chance you might be able to contribute to this piece of work. This
immersion naturally lets expectations, hopes, and fears fade away; none
of it matters. Treating your work like a craft will help you let go of external
measures of quality and focus on what's in front of you. Everything else is
an unnecessary distraction.

22. https://www.nytimes.com/2009/01/11/opinion/11bono.html

Whenever a thought of comparison comes across your mind, notice it, and then let go. If you catch yourself ruminating about it, tap it away like a feather duster cleaning a glass and bring your mind back to whatever you are doing. As composer, band leader, and saxophonist Charlie Parker said, "Don't play the saxophone. Let it play you."

↪ **Or flip this prompt:** *Make Them Curious*[§10.4]

6.6 *Enjoy the Plateau*

Mastering any skill, including all forms of creative work, means spending a lot of time moving forward slowly. The spurts of growth are very occasional, perhaps even rare. Instead, day in and day out, we are working. We are practicing. "At the heart of it, mastery is practice. Mastery is staying on the path," writes martial artist and author George Leonard.

Make your practice enjoyable. Don't obsess over improving, or whether someone else is better or worse than you in some way. Stay focused on your own skill set and craft. Perhaps it means changing your environment or schedule. It could also mean switching the routine or the sources of inspiration.

If you find yourself wrestling with metrics such as likes, shares, and comments, check out why three creators ignore the stats[§13.3] and some alternate ways of measuring success. You can also choose to set a mission[§13.2] for your work.

6.7 *Relax Expectations*

With vision[§13.4] comes expectations. We believe *this* project will be the one that enables us to break through. It would be weird if we didn't—there might be less of a point in working on it. This expectation can serve as an occasional fuel, but more often gets in the way of us doing our best work. It's where many creative blocks start.

"It's important to keep the ideas going. A lot of times, you can't get too worried about the results. I'm in a business where basically I get hired and fired as soon as a song comes out," Dacoury Natche told me in an interview for this book.

Chris Kim, who produces music under the name CVRE, is known best for making songs with artists like Justin Bieber, Future, and Don Toliver. Based on his wide range of musical experiences, he observed to me, "Expectation always kills creativity. ... You expect a certain result and you have to achieve that industrial definition of success that always kills the magic that could happen in the unknown."

If you feel your expectations rising, that this project you're working on is going to be a hit, acknowledge that there's a chance it might also just be another project. The external measures of success might come after the next one, or the one after that. That is the beauty of consistency. You always have another shot. Another opportunity is just around the corner if you want it to be.

Keeping your expectations modest will ensure that you cultivate the consistency you need not only to improve, but to make an impact. As recording artist Pharrell Williams said,[23] "I never feel anxious about anything. Why would I? If I felt anxious or put pressure on myself then nothing would be fun."

6.8 *Relinquish Results*

Throughout the years, we are conditioned to do things well and to constantly improve. If we're not doing that, we're led to believe we're getting worse. If we regress, we are failures. These beliefs are all based on the flawed assumption that progress is linear.

At an extreme, this could lead us to chase perfection. If we can't do something perfectly, we just won't do it. Perfectionism creates an impossible standard for us to meet. This is just one of many reasons we start procrastinating and get blocked.

In his book *Surely You're Joking, Mr. Feynman!*, Nobel Prize-winning physicist Richard Feynman recalls an art class when he was instructed to draw without looking at the paper. He was impressed with the results, noticing a "funny, semi-Picasso like strength" in his work. He knew that it would be impossible to draw well without looking at the paper, so he didn't consciously try. He writes, "I had thought that 'loosen up' meant 'make sloppy drawings,' but it really meant to relax and not worry about how the

---

23. https://www.vogue.co.uk/article/born-lucky

drawing is going to come out." The solution is to do something without caring about the results.

The immediate goal is for you to take a very small step closer to the thing you want to do. You already know your form's most essential element;[§6.1] now it's time to build something with it. If you want to write a book, then write at least one sentence in a notebook today, building up to a daily writing practice. If you want to draw, sketch out a person or an object—don't think too hard, just choose something in front of you and draw. If you want to make music, hum a melody into the voice memo in your phone and try to create it on an instrument or in your computer.

If you're uncertain, then follow the first thing that pops into your head after 30 seconds. Or do the thing you think you want to do. Or do the thing you think your best friend thinks you want to do. Or write a list out[§8.1] and roll dice.[§8.3] Don't make your goal to "finish a thing"; make it to "start with anything." By design, the task should never impose on your schedule. It should be small enough that you can do it within a minute or two. That short time makes it difficult to do anything well, so hopefully you will put that possibility out of your mind and focus on the process. There will be a time and place to care about results—but it's not while you do the work.

PART II: FROM ACTION COMES PROGRESS

"Draw, Antonio, draw and don't waste time."

— Michelangelo[24]

When we were children, none of us needed to be told to draw.[25] It was practically primal. We would naturally doodle. Yet at some point, most of us stop drawing. Comedian and writer Ricky Gervais quoted[26] Pablo Picasso saying,[27] "Every child is an artist. The problem is how to remain an artist once he grows up." While the popular quote remains unverified, it's not difficult to imagine the words coming out of Picasso's mouth. John Lennon said something similar:[28] "Every child is an artist until he's told he's not an artist."

Human beings have an instinct to create, but we are made to unlearn it, suppress it, and repress it as we grow up. Our natural-born instinct to be creative, to play, and to look at the world with wonder and limitless possibility is stifled and tamped down so we can deal with the unpleasant business of being adults. A lifetime of comments like "You can't do that," "That's not how things work," and "Do you have a backup plan?" beat us into thinking practically and logically.

While the more analytical side of our minds—the judge[§5.6]—is great for lots of things, we can't count on it to think our way into being more creative. The solution is not to try to think our way out of this, but to take action and to let the brain follow. "If you want to think differently, first learn to act differently," scientist Heinz von Foerster said.

---

24. https://www.apollo-magazine.com/how-to-learn-drawing-from-michelangelo/

25. https://web.archive.org/web/20201127012418/www.bookslut.com/features/2009_07_014748
    .php

26. https://web.archive.org/web/20120129233514/http://www.wired.co.uk/news/archive/
    2011-10/05/ricky-gervais-twitter

27. https://twitter.com/rickygervais/status/120431149817405440

28. https://quoteinvestigator.com/2015/03/07/child-art/

Figure: Le Penseur by Auguste Rodin, in the Rodin museum in Paris. Credit: שעש, Wikimedia Commons.[29]

The Musée Rodin in Paris exhibits one of 27 known variations of a bronze sculpture entitled *Le Penseur*—the Thinker—by sculptor Auguste Rodin. The figure is sitting on a rock, hunched over, its hand cradling its chin, and its eyes staring at the ground. Such is the archetypal image of the thinker, which has influenced how we imagine any form of thought,

29. https://commons.wikimedia.org/wiki/File:Le_Penseur1.jpg

including creative thinking. A modern image of the thinker would still split up the act of engaging our intellectual abilities from movement and senses, though probably in a more luxurious post—say, in an expensive ergonomic swivel chair, or lying down on a chesterfield sofa.

What this image doesn't express is the fact that we actually learn and process thought while we move and take action. Action generates creative breakthroughs. One person who embodied this insight worked just across from *Le Penseur* at the Musée Rodin, on the other side of the Seine, at the head offices of Louis Vuitton. He wouldn't often be caught sitting and staring at the ground; for many years, he didn't even have a desk at his own office.

The late Virgil Abloh started his fashion career not by sitting around thinking about fashion, but by visiting a screen-printing shop and printing a design he made with Adobe Illustrator on a T-shirt. As his solo work grew more popular (he was previously best known for being creative assistant to Ye, who at the time went by Kanye West), Abloh said[30] all of the ensuing opportunities came "from a moment that happened four years earlier in which I took an idea and got it made." This comment was prescient; several years after he got the T-shirt printed and completed many more creative projects, Louis Vuitton would appoint Virgil Abloh to be its artistic director of menswear. Abloh's brand Off-White would break through mainstream culture and get acquired by Louis Vuitton's parent company LVMH.

Rewinding back before the accolades, that moment where Abloh got the first T-shirt printed happened in the midst of him supporting Ye through one of his most productive periods—after *My Beautiful Dark Twisted Fantasy*, during the *Watch the Throne* recording process and accompanying tour, and during the *Cruel Summer* compilation album. Even in this busy time, Abloh found a way to make it happen. He said, "Go and print that T-shirt today, and by today I mean in the next 30 minutes. If you don't do it, that's your problem."

Abloh's friend, creative director Justin Saunders, said to GQ,[31] "What I knew about creativity was saying no to things, but he's on the opposite flip. It's like when Virgil convinced me to be a DJ—I still don't know how to use a mixer. I said to Virgil, 'I don't know how to DJ,' and he said, 'It doesn't

30. https://i-d.vice.com/en_us/article/evnqm4/
creation-curation-and-collaboration-virgil-abloh39s-remixed-world-us-translation

31. https://www.gq.com/story/virgil-abloh-cover-story-spring-2019

matter. Let's just go have some fun.' And then eventually we were DJ'ing at Coachella."

Abloh's instinct is, in some ways, innate in each of us. While we know that action doesn't necessarily produce immediate results, it has a tendency to make *something* happen. To artist Sarah Lucas,[32] creative breakthroughs happen spontaneously and suddenly, creating greater progress than her hours or days of slogging through hard work. But upon reflection, she wonders if maybe they happened as an indirect result of, or relief from, her hard work.

You get lucky as you keep moving along and learning. Or, perhaps, it's more true to say that your unluckiness runs out. If you have to wait until you're sure of what's going to happen before you take action, you could be waiting forever. Even if you believe that circumstance, fortune, and fate control the majority of your life, you still have choices to make about the small parts you control.

Our actions train our brains to think, using our bodies. They also train our brains to see the opportunities for progress. Graphic designer Milton Glaser, who created the iconic "I ❤ NY" logo, says in an interview, "What happens with the brain is that the more you do something, the more deep those impulses become."

Leonardo da Vinci called this "componimento inculto," which biographer Walter Isaacson describes as "an uncultivated composition that helps work out ideas through an intuitive process." Basically, thinking by sketching.

The first two chapters will enable us to get back in touch with our inner artists by finding the energy, and inspiration, to make a vast quantity of acceptable work. Then, we'll keep working but begin to focus on defining and developing the quality of our work. In the final two chapters, we'll take steps to share our work and learn from others.

---

32. https://subtlemaneuvers.substack.com/p/john-ashberys-writing-process-was

7 Make Constraints Your Canvas

In *The Craftsman,* author Richard Sennett tells the story of two houses. The first is the work of philosopher Ludwig Wittgenstein, who financed the design and construction of his house with his virtually limitless family fortune. He set out with his eye on perfection, eager to build the prototype of "the foundations of all possible buildings." His integrity could spare no expense. Stuart Jeffries writes in the *Guardian,*[33] "When the house was nearly complete, he insisted that a ceiling be raised 30 mm so that the proportions he wanted (3:1, 3:2, 2:1) were perfectly executed."

33. https://www.theguardian.com/books/2002/jan/05/arts.highereducation

Figure: Villa Müller by Adolf Loos in Prague-Střešovice, Czech Republic. Credit: Miaow Miaow, Wikimedia Commons.[34]

One of Wittgenstein's mentors and friends, the more senior Adolf Loos, had a smaller purse to draw from. When the foundations of his Villa Müller were set differently from the plan, he thickened a side wall to accommodate the change. His two choices were to adapt or to give up on the building.

Loos's Villa Müller was built on necessity and constraint, twin mischiefs that drained it of all potential for perfection. Sennett writes, "The formally pure properties of the [Villa Müller] were achieved by working with many similar mistakes and impediments Loos had to take as facts on the ground; necessity stimulated his sense of form." Villa Müller has remained a cultural icon through the decades. In the late 90s, the Prague government invested a million dollars into restoring it[35] to its original form.

But after Wittgenstein's house was complete, he called his own creation "sickened." He is quoted[36] saying, "But *primordial* life, wild life

34. https://commons.wikimedia.org/wiki/File:Villa_Muller_054.jpg

35. http://www.harvarddesignmagazine.org/issues/15/white-walls-in-the-golden-city

36. https://ndpr.nd.edu/news/
    dialectic-of-the-ladder-wittgenstein-the-tractatus-and-modernism/

striving to erupt into the open—that is lacking. And so you could say it isn't *healthy.*" His sister Gretl's nephew sold the house on the grounds that she never liked it. Wittgenstein's other sister, Hermine, confessed to not wanting to live in it. Ludwig Wittgenstein's obsession with perfection bore rotten fruit.

Creativity comes from chaotic energy. But left unchecked, the chaotic energy is a breeding ground for obsession, fixation, and compulsiveness. Constraints provide the structure that creativity needs in order to come into the real world. Think back to Professor Betty Flowers's image of the madman[§5.6]—chaotic energy—and the judge—structure. Philosopher Friedrich Nietzsche writes in *The Birth of Tragedy*[37] of a similar blend of halves to achieve balance: the Dionysian extremes of emotion, instinct, and spontaneity, and the Apollonian rationality, order, and reason.

In Wittgenstein's case, his practically infinite capabilities overcame his sense of constraints, allowing his chaotic side to run wild, unchecked by any realistic force except gravity, throwing the halves out of balance. Even though giving in to chaotic energy might feel good, it doesn't necessarily make for better final work.

"Your creativity needs enough structure to support your freedom, but not so much that your freedom feels stifled," says Lindsay Jean Thomson. The ideal balance is different for everyone, and it also changes with time. These prompts will support you in finding the constraints that work for you, right now.

7.1 *Select One Tool*

Professor, author, and human-technology researcher Sherry Turkle suggests in *The Empathy Diaries*, "To be good at a job, you had to love the objects associated with that job." This can also apply to your chosen creative operation.[§5.1] Finding an object that sparks joy could change how you operate.

For example, Big Mike's current journey with painting started off with a canvas he found across the street from his workplace. Even if this lucky event hadn't happened, I can imagine him buying a canvas and paints and getting started painting the same day. He didn't let himself get stuck figur-

---

37. https://www.gutenberg.org/files/51356/51356-h/51356-h.htm

ing out which paints were best, which brush to use, where he could work. His method, in his own words, is simple: "Put the paint on the canvas!"

Choosing a tool provides you with a clear idea of what you will be doing. You paint with a paintbrush. You draw or write with a pencil. Commit to this tool for a set amount of time—maybe 10 days[§7.5]—just enough time to see what you can do with it but not so much that you get bored.

Don't overthink the tool just yet.[§5.2] Start with the simplest version of the tool, the one you already have lying around, and figure out what you need out of it along the way. As Wired co-founder Kevin Kelly writes,[38] "Start by buying the absolute cheapest tools you can find. Upgrade the ones you use a lot. If you wind up using some tool for a job, buy the very best you can afford."

7.2 *Set a Time Limit*

In 2018, the average Instagram user on Android spent 53 minutes a day on Instagram.[39] Over the course of the year, that's 322 hours, the equivalent of over eight full 40-hour work weeks.

Imagine what you could create with 53 minutes a day! (Especially if you're reclaiming that time from Instagram.) Even five minutes will move you further along your creative path than no minutes at all. You can begin to reclaim time for creative work by setting yourself a manageable limit.

You can use a technique called *timeboxing*, which means giving yourself a set amount of time to do one thing. One of my favorite devices is the kitchen timer. I've bought maybe a dozen of these in my life so far, and I plan to buy dozens more. I set the timer for a few minutes—for a short workout, for a sprint through really boring paperwork, or to get started on a big creative project—and then I press start. I give myself a window to work through. After that, I can choose to stop, and sometimes I do. But many other times, I keep going.

In the professional world, a popular productivity strategy is the Pomodoro method: set a timer for 25 minutes of uninterrupted time to complete a task, take a five-minute break, then start the timer again. After

---

38. https://kk.org/thetechnium/68-bits-of-unsolicited-advice/

39. https://www.vox.com/2018/6/25/17501224/
    instagram-facebook-snapchat-time-spent-growth-data

three of these 25 minute sessions, the person takes a longer 30-minute break.

A deadline is a variation of this time constraint. In her memoir *Bossypants*, producer and actor Tina Fey quotes *Saturday Night Live* creator Lorne Michaels: "The show doesn't go on because it's ready; it goes on because it's 11:30." You can set a deadline and timed event to happen regularly: "Every day when I wake up, I'm going to take two minutes and write a note." You might also challenge yourself to make something whenever you have idle time, like when you're waiting for a bus or during commercial breaks. You won't find inspiration by waiting for it;[§8.2] you'll need to put the work in to uncover it. And you don't only do creative work when you're inspired, you do it because it's on your schedule to do it.

7.3 *Commit to a Size*

The two most common dimensions we're constrained by are space and time. If setting a time limit is timeboxing, then perhaps the space-analogous exercise can be called *sizeboxing*. You pick a limited size for your work and work within that.

One popular format I've seen is an essay that fits in a screenshot on your phone. When working on articles, I write my notes to fit a 4-by-6-inch index card; any longer and it has to be a new note. This keeps me concise.

If you're recording music, scale down by committing to recording a song with only two instruments if you usually use more; or if you want to produce a lot of ideas, commit to writing thirty-second melodies for one week.

If you're working with paint, choose a surface with dimensions no more than four inches by four inches.

If you're programming, restrict yourself to a set number of lines of code or a specific memory size. (Sizecoding[40] might be an inspiration.)

Another version of this is filling out three pages of writing in a notebook. (If you do this without stopping, that's what teacher, artist, and author Julia Cameron calls the morning pages.[41])

The less time you have, the smaller a size—or the fewer the elements[§8.3]—that you may want to go with.

---

40. https://www.sizecoding.org/

41. https://juliacameronlive.com/basic-tools/morning-pages/

7.4 *Do Your Work without Your Equipment*

While most of the prompts in this book involve getting ideas out of your head and into the world by taking action, and creating ideas through action, this prompt is about working on an idea in your head and leaving your studio, laptop, or gear bag behind. Steve Jobs said,[42] "Creativity is just connecting things."

These connections come from many sources, including what you see and experience. Photographer Ivan Chow leaves the house without his camera[43] to practice his observation skills. He says, "By taking away the need to make photos, you're relieving yourself of that pressure to deliver. This will allow your mind to focus solely on spotting moments that are worthy of capturing. You'll get less caught up with what's directly in front of you and you'll start looking a bit further to spot potential subjects and points of interest. Being a good street photographer is all about being good at observing, and that means that you already have a very good head start."

If your chosen creative operation is photography, you might choose to take a moment out of each day to observe a location or scene that would make for an interesting photograph. What makes it stand out to you? How can you return and recreate the moment, or would it be worth capturing in different lighting conditions? If it's music, take a long walk and play with a melody in your head—when you take away the option of recording an idea right away, you're forced to work with the raw materials in real time, which can lead to many surprising developments.

Working without equipment can also help us stay connected to our creativity when we can't access resources. Shawn "Jay-Z" Carter memorized lyrics during the early moments of his career, as he writes in a piece for *Vibe*. "When my thoughts began to crowd each other, I would go to the corner store, get a pen, and empty my head, pouring rhymes onto pieces of paper bags. But how many scraps can you fit in your pocket? I had to start memorizing my ideas until I got home, which was usually in the wee hours of the morning. Ironically, using memorization to hold on to my lines is the way I developed the writing style I use today. No pen, paper, or paper bags needed. Just point out the track and I'm all over it."

---

42. https://www.wired.com/1996/02/jobs-2/

43. https://www.youtube.com/watch?v=Er891QANmRs

This is what Michael Saviello says of his process: "I do a painting in a short amount of time, but I think about it 24 hours." Saviello paints from still images, so this is a natural part of his process; he might have an image in mind but change the background or other elements. You can work mentally—consider different variations of your final product and change the structure, or the order, and imagine how it turns out. This helps to keep ideas accessible in your conscious mind, and to let the unconscious side of your brain work on them.

But whatever you come up with in that great brain of yours, don't forget to record it, write it down, etc. As Jay-Z acknowledged about his early, equipment-less process to NPR,[44] "I've lost plenty of material. It's not the best way. I wouldn't advise it to anyone. I've lost a couple albums' worth of great material. ... Think about when you can't remember a word and it drives you crazy. So imagine forgetting an entire rhyme. 'What's that? I said I was the greatest something?'"

↦ **Or flip this prompt:** *Make Idle Time*$^{\S 6.3}$

7.5 *Set a 10-Day Quota*

The mystique of art and creativity shines a spotlight on inspiration and creative breakthroughs. A practitioner will speak more of the power of repetition, routine, and tangible deliverables.

This is a priceless lesson that many people have paid thousands of dollars in tuition to learn. As I share in Source Inspiration,$^{\S 8.2}$ graphic designer and Pentagram partner Michael Bierut assigned a project to his students: pick an activity and commit to doing it for 100 days in a row. Bierut recalls his instructions:[45] "The only restrictions on the operation you choose is that it must be repeated in some form every day, and that every iteration must be documented for eventual presentation." Bierut would repeat this project in each class in the following years. One student chose to dance every day, another chose to make a poster in under 60 seconds each day, and still another made a different version of the same poster each day.

---

44. https://www.npr.org/2010/11/16/131334322/the-fresh-air-interview-jay-z-decoded
45. https://designobserver.com/feature/five-years-of-100-days/24678

This is a reliable way to gain experience, improve your skills, and build discipline. Lindsay Jean Thomson, who facilitates the 100 Day Project, an online project inspired by Bierut's class, told me in an interview that there is a noticeable improvement in how the projects turn out from day one to day 100. "If you sit down and do something every day, you *will* get better at it," she says.

One hundred days can sound like too much of a commitment, so I suggest starting with 10. If you feel on day 10 that it's manageable, then continue to day 100.

You have innate discipline; it might just be asleep. The daily quota will cultivate this discipline, channeling it into your creative work, until it's strong enough to take over and it becomes a part of who you are.

For added accountability, participants in the 100 Day Project need to share their progress every day on Instagram, and Bierut's students presented their project at the end of the 100 days. To keep yourself accountable, I'd recommend doing the same form of public documentation during this 10-day project. If you find that the work isn't ready for you to show to all of your followers yet, find a friend or classmate who might want to share their own 10-day project with you. Now you have an accountability partner.

The beauty of this exercise is that it also encourages you to find idle time[§6.3] and space in your day for your creative work, helping you form creative habits that will last well after this 10- or 100-day project is complete.

↦ **Or flip this prompt:** *Do the Opposite*[§8.4]

7.6 *Choose Analog*

Before he became the Grammy-winning DJ Dahi, Dacoury Natche used to play, practice, and experiment with instruments. It was how he became a musician. As he gained success in his industry, more and more of his work was done on a computer. "So much of what I was doing just felt rigid because I'm stuck within a screen," said Natche. As a response, he remembered what he temporarily forgot—that he used to make music outside of his screen, with instruments.

Using only analog equipment—nothing connected to the internet—practice your craft. Make something. Going back to basics can be a great way to revisit why you chose this work in the first place, as Natche describes. It's a chance for us to let go of the constraints and systems we need in order to work with technology, and to remember the simplest elements of the craft.[6.1]

7.7 *Complete Your Operation in Seconds*

Social scientist B.J. Fogg's Behavioral Model[46] tells us that the more ability a task requires, the more motivation it will also require. That idea can certainly apply to creative work, which is why these prompts require minimal ability and time. This insight is key to creating habits and tapping into your discipline.

Vin Verma, who goes by the name Internetvin, has made music[47] and written code[48] every day for a year. One of his techniques is to find a way to create music or code in 20 seconds (writing just a single line of code[49] on the days he didn't have time or felt tired).

If you're making music, your tactic could be to record a 10-second voice note of a new melody, or to write one bad line of a song lyric.

If you're working in photography, take a still life of an object within arm's reach.

If you're writing, write one bad sentence.

The goal here is to simplify your creative operation, moving the starting point to the finish point much closer together—mere seconds apart.

While 20 seconds is an aspirational goal, realistically it may take at least a minute to complete the simplest version of your creative operation. If you're writing every day, let it take a minute to write a sentence. Or if you're drawing daily, then a minute enables you to quickly sketch something simple.

This prompt can also stack up well with setting a 10-day quota.[7.5] For example, I wrote a constrained comic for ten days, which consisted of one drawing and four panels. On the first day, I spent no more than an hour drawing the character and duplicating it across four panels. The next nine

46. https://www.behaviormodel.org/
47. https://twitter.com/internetvin/status/1019033516028280832
48. https://twitter.com/internetvin/status/1212501595403014147
49. https://web.archive.org/web/20200103101837/https://twitter.com/internetVin/status/1212501604156526595

days, I simply copied the panels and changed the dialogue. Here's what one of them looks like:

Mike Winkelmann, known as Beeple, has made an original illustration every day for over a decade. He ordinarily spends a couple of hours each day, but he still spent a few minutes on the days[50] he had food poisoning and even on the day his child was born.

Life gets busy sometimes. The trick is to find ways to keep the habit going in a matter of seconds or minutes. On days where you have little time to spare, this short, small, variation will make sure you keep progressing.

---

50. https://www.vice.com/en_us/article/78g539/beeple-cgi-master-10-years-everydays-results

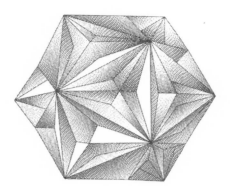

8 Never Run Out of Ideas

It's tempting to believe that "ideas" are what you wait for, sitting quietly until inspiration strikes. Ideas can come down on us in this way, but more commonly, creators and artists cultivate their own inspiration by recording as many possibilities as they can come up with, generating their own idea momentum.

Not every idea has to be good—some ideas will be horrendous. But the consistent work of generating ideas, good or bad, relevant or not, is what matters in developing creative thinking. The point is to discover just how possible it is to *make* ideas every day, not just "have" them whenever the gods decide.

Creating acceptable ideas is a strategy that professor and author Dean Keith Simonton recommends. He writes in *The Genius Checklist* how the more attempts an artist or craftsperson makes, the more major works (or "hits") they create. As a general rule, Simonton suggests that mass production of these ideas is a safer approach than focusing on a single idea and trying to make it perfect.

"Giving up on perfectionism doesn't mean that you will not produce anything perfect, but rather that perfection will happen from time to time because of the sheer mass of output," Simonton writes. Throughout their lives, some artists have made this prolific approach work. Famous examples include Yayoi Kusama's 9,000 pieces, Shantell Martin's 5,000 works, Wolfgang Amadeus Mozart's 800 compositions, Pablo Picasso's 20,000 drawings, and Vincent van Gogh's 2,000 drawings as examples of this strategy.

8.1 *Write Down 10 Ideas*

Virgil Abloh told i-D Magazine[51] in 2015 that he came up with 30 ideas a day. Just for fun, here's an example of what one of them looked like:

Source: Off-White Imaginary TV on Instagram.[52]

If you're like me, 30 ideas will take you two hours—so I decided to start with a more modest 10.

You can write down or draw out any idea you like. If your interest is in architecture or interior design and you want to design a house, drawing it out counts as an idea. Even if you consider yourself a writer, and you

51. https://i-d.vice.com/en_uk/article/evnqm4/
    creation-curation-and-collaboration-virgil-ablohs-remixed-world
52. https://www.instagram.com/p/CC8U17UFsN6/

have an idea for an app, write it down. That counts. If your friend has told you that the two of you should throw a party, write it down. You can use an existing reference and circle design elements you would have decided to change. You can write down a one-sentence response to something you read. What was the most interesting thing you read yesterday? What can't you not stop thinking about? What was the coolest thing you saw yesterday? What was the most interesting thing you heard about? What is a different version of something you just made? Can you remix one of the things you saw, heard, or learned yesterday?

Write it down!

An idea can appear in point form, it can be a drawing, it can be one line, your eyes may be open or they may be closed. And you can apply whatever constraint you like to these ideas.

You may be surprised at how many ideas are forming or present in your mind all the time. Here's an example of what one day's ideas looked like for me, exactly as I wrote them (Canadian spellings included):

1. *Sponsoring or buying a product as a way of buying into someone's future. This reminds me of a podcast from WorkOS who had said the same thing.*

2. *Enterprise animals—animals that make jokes about IT sysadmin, etc...*

3. *My writing as a combination of Shea Serrano (because he's so versatile he can write about anything in culture!) and ... ??? See Byrne Hobart's description of his own intersection in Marker non huckster piece*

4. *I add value as an idea generator (because I've been exposed to so many through reading)—and how I'm giving a lot away because there's no way I can actually do all of these ideas. And that's what Virgil [Abloh] did too, I think. You need to have the ideas to provide direction—or you're executing them. That's what high level means... see the book on hierarchy*

5. *DM interviews—just interview Twitter-famous people on DM/iMessage/Signal or over email for my blog, and let them know I also republish at Medium with 12k+ followers and sometimes at Fast Company as well. This should take no more than 30 mins on my end, and I can set up templated questions*

just like I do with Crossing the Enterprise Chasm. *They can respond in text*

6. *Marketing as training your brain to see opportunity and optimism, which is what sets expectations too*

7. *Tourist, purist, and traveller. The value of the traveller is they bring a global perspective, a "holistic" one—they are a purist in their own way, the way of globalization. Tyler Brule is one. Virgil was one too!*

8. *"Best practices"—doing a lot of stuff and seeing what works and what doesn't. Based on hypotheses, thinking, and guiding principles of course because nobody can do everything. "Allow strategy to emerge."*

9. *Singapore real estate isn't an asset, art ownership as home ownership, and a world where art is handled as an asset like real estate*

10. *Print the comics out in newsprint or some other unique type of paper and then take the photo. There is something curious about the screen–paper–screen transition. One of many ideas that emerged from French Dispatch.*

It's messy, practically in scribbles, and that's the way it's supposed to be. Seriously, you can write these ideas down wherever you like—in a napkin, on your hand, in your notebook, in a spreadsheet. I like to write mine down in my phone, or whatever pen and paper I can find, and keep track of them$^{\S5.5}$ in Airtable, so I can search them up later. I sort them by reverse chronological order, and whenever I think of an old idea, I find it, add to it, and move it back up to the top.

You don't need to work on these ideas right away. It's tempting to get swept away by the chaos of inspiration, and haphazardly throw new routines and processes into the mix, but it's important, even with new ideas, to know why you're trying something new. Coming up with new ideas won't matter if you're not able to bring any of them into reality. You may find you need to write the ideas down and save them for later in order for you to truly focus on verifying one and bringing it to life.

8.2 *Source Inspiration*

One of the most difficult parts of creative work is sitting down and deciding what to actually do. One solution to that is to draw from a predefined source, each day. For example, over a decade after he first worked as a lecturer at Yale, graphic designer and Pentagram partner Michael Bierut assigned a brand new project to his students: pick an activity and commit to doing it for 100 days in a row.[§7.5] This project emerged from a practice that Bierut had started five years prior to the assignment, starting January 1, 2002.

Every day, Bierut would make one interpretive drawing of a photo he found in the *New York Times*. These drawings could take just a few minutes, perhaps even a matter of seconds. They could also be more elaborate, if he had the time. But no matter what, he never ran out of ideas—because every day the *New York Times* came out, he would get more. You're free to do what Bierut did, which is to pick a source that provides a constant stream of new ideas.

You could also choose to train your attention, by taking photos of an object that you like anytime you see it in your life. Virgil Abloh observed an acquaintance taking a photo every time he saw a specific luxury handbag, which essentially trained his mind to see it during his day-to-day life. Abloh said,[53] "If you want to find new space, if you want to get to another crescendo of design, and having your brain figure out how to aesthetically put together something, you have to do it often." You could also do this with visual patterns, as Abloh did with diagonal stripes.[54]

If you prefer writing fiction, you could respond to the r/WritingPrompts[55] subreddit, which surfaces new prompts every day. If you're more interested in nonfiction or memoir writing, you can try author and speaker Suleika Jaouad's The Isolation Journals.[56]

You could also prepare a set of sources. For example, before Bierut's student Zak Klauck started doing his 60-second posters, he had put together 100 phrases (some from friends, others he selected on his own) to design from. That meant the 60 seconds could be spent working on the actual poster, not finding a source or thinking of what to do.

---

53. https://www.youtube.com/watch?v=qie5VITX6eQ

54. https://www.complex.com/style/2016/07/off-white-virgil-abloh-branding-diagonal-lines

55. https://www.reddit.com/r/WritingPrompts/

56. https://www.theisolationjournals.com/explore?offset=1586170800649

If you want to learn more, I've compiled a comprehensive list of 25 daily creative challenges[57] at my blog.

8.3 *Roll the Dice*

Letting go of control, and introducing chaos into an environment, is one of the keys to cultivating creativity. If you're ever experiencing blockage or a sense of stuckness on a decision, try opening the door to chance in order to support your creative work.

In *The Travels and Adventures of Serendipity*,[58] authors Robert K. Merton and Elinor Barber quote the late Professor Salvador Luria of the University of Illinois as praising "controlled sloppiness, which states that it often pays to do somewhat untidy experiments, provided one is aware of the element of untidiness." In any case, the idea here is to trend toward chaos, entropy, and randomness in your work—a sense of controlled sloppiness.

For example, if you're feeling stuck on what to write, you can take a chance with a dictionary or a random word generator. In literature, there is a constrained writing movement called Oulipo. Several of their techniques are set by constraints and involve chance. For example, the N+7 technique involves creating a new poem through taking an existing poem and replacing each noun with the seventh noun after it in the dictionary. In the 1920s artistic movement Dada, a common game to manufacture inspiration involved cutting up newspapers and pulling words and sentences out of a bag.[59]

In the board game Letter Tycoon, each player starts their turn with a limited set of vowels and consonants, with the goal of spelling out the highest scoring words. You could replicate this game by picking eight letters and write as many words as you can with the set as possible. If you're feeling ambitious, you can even compose a poem or write a sentence with the letters.

---

57. https://herbertlui.net/daily-creative-challenges-creativity-activity/

58. https://press.princeton.edu/books/paperback/9780691126302/
the-travels-and-adventures-of-serendipity

59. https://www.writing.upenn.edu/~afilreis/88v/tzara.html

A popular improvisational comedy technique is the one word story, which requires two or more people. The goal is to tell a story by taking turns, each person adding one word at a time.

Similarly, in *The Creative Habit*, legendary choreographer and author Twyla Tharp shares an exercise where she throws a group of coins on a table. Based on how they land, she draws ideas from the arrangement, occasionally rearranging some of them to be in a more pleasing pattern.

Anytime you experience reluctance at leaving something up to chance, consider that Donald Glover developed his stage name, Childish Gambino, through a Wu-Tang Clan name generator.[60] (He has succeeded perhaps in spite of the name, saying,[61] "If I had known it was going to be something for real, I wouldn't have used it." The lesson I chose to take is there's perfect vision only in hindsight, and you can make mistakes and still get to where you want to go!)

Chance plays a huge role in creativity and can be a useful generative constraint. If you want to make fewer decisions, enlist chance as an assistant. Whenever you need to make a decision, write out your options and let a coin toss, a dice roll, a results generator,[62] or another person's selection of multiple choice, to decide what you'll do.

8.4 *Do the Opposite*

Whatever your routine is, flip it.

A friend once told me, "If you keep doing what you've done, you'll keep getting what you've gotten." I wrote this down, though I probably didn't need to; it has continued boomeranging back into my brain throughout the years. Sometimes, in order to make breakthroughs or to disrupt our patterns, we need to flip our habits, routines, and rituals on their heads. Similar to rolling the dice,[§8.3] this is about opening the door to chaos to introduce new creative ideas.

Even if what you're doing is getting you the results you want, it's almost always worth trying something new in a small way (unless a process is in a critical stage of a project with high stakes—for example, you probably don't want to change the way you fire up a kiln for a project

60. https://wutangclan.net/name-generator/
61. https://www.youtube.com/watch?v=gU1sTWIbw_
62. https://www.randomresult.com/

you'd spent the past four months on). You're creating an opportunity to get better results,[63] or different ones. I discovered this saying through author Neal Pasricha's book *You Are Awesome*: "Different is better than better." Author Laura Huang writes a different version in her book *Edge*: "Different isn't always better, but better is always different."

"If you get so good at drawing with your right hand that you can even make a beautiful sketch with your eyes closed, you should immediately change to your left hand to avoid repeating yourself," Marina Abramović quotes artist Krsto Hegedušić in her memoir, *Walk Through Walls*. In this case, you could try drawing for a few minutes with your eyes closed as Abramović suggests, and as Richard Feynman did.[§6.8] You could also try drawing with your non-dominant hand. If you like what you see, you could expand the time to an entire work session. The writer's equivalent might be working on a piece of fiction if you've only ever written essays.

If you do your creative work in the morning, try doing it for an hour or two at night. One of my high school teachers had actually recommended waking up in the middle of the night to write.[64] Interrupting sleep is certainly not pleasant, though the creative work you produce by shaking up your routine might be worth it.

If you start your creative process with meticulous outlines and sketches (as I do!), try doing the final version as soon as possible—even in a single work session. I find the time compression equal parts stimulating and exciting. Even though I end the session dissatisfied with the so-called final draft, I often look back and realize that it wasn't as bad as I had thought. Conversely, if you're used to completing your work in a day, take a week, or a month, to do it.

In addition to experimenting with time, you can also find an opposing space for one work session. If you usually work in large, open spaces, try finding one that's extremely small (channeling your inner Jackson Pollock, who worked in a relatively modest studio, or Roald Dahl's backyard hut). Conversely, if you usually work in a small space, try working in a big place, like the foyer of a public library or even outdoors.

---

63. https://forge.medium.com/to-make-a-breakthrough-flip-your-routine-29eec3e7f5a3?sk=6ee374e5cf5f1035513d2155e4a25a83

64. https://www.bbc.com/future/article/20220107-the-lost-medieval-habit-of-biphasic-sleep

Creativity means walking a tightrope between consistency and chaos. Switch up your routines so that you naturally add more novelty and vitality to your work.

↬ **Or flip this prompt:** *Set a 10-Day Quota*[§7.5]

8.5 *Turn Problems Into Ideas*

Many of these prompts have been akin to *invention*: making ideas and trying new things. In *Let My People Go Surfing*, Patagonia founder Yvon Chouinard writes about how his company doesn't invent—it discovers. "There's simply no time for inventing," he writes. Instead, the company talks directly to customers and learns how they use its products. The company digitally renders new ideas, makes samples, and works to shorten the time it takes to implement these changes. From those situations, Patagonia finds guidance on how its products evolve. Of course, this involves developing an understanding of people and providing them with a solution.

Your idea can be a solution. For example, if you've heard a friend talk about how boring their new apartment or house is, you can paint something that gently alleviates some of that boredom or something so bold it completely shatters it. If you're a programmer hearing someone talk about their problems with gardening, you can build a simple app to help solve them.

8.6 *Focus on Connection*

This prompt is about making something just for one person, someone you know, as a way of finding authentic creative expression. Productivity writer Tim Ferriss found the tone for his books[65] when drafting an email to his best friend. Michelle Kuo, assigns letters to all of her students, whether it's in classes at The American University of Paris or at a creative workshop for incarcerated people. She observes when people begin to write, they risk their voices sounding pretentious, because it's common to believe "good writing" means impenetrable or abstruse. Kuo told me, "There's

65. https://tim.blog/2018/02/06/
the-tim-ferriss-show-transcripts-the-4-hour-workweek-revisited/

something about writing a letter that allows you to discover your conversational voice, which also means your forms of speech, your idioms, your little jokes. Sometimes, it also allows the voice to be funnier, to be self deprecating, and to desire actual connection. When a person knows who their exact audience is, it gives them more consistency, so they're not switching between different potential targets. When you're consistent, then the reader trusts you. An outside reader trusts you."

Kuo suggests that if you're into songwriting or the recording arts, an equivalent to the letter could be a ballad. Bernice Liu, also known as artist Spime, suggests a visual equivalent could be a signed painting or a portrait of someone you know.

One happy byproduct of focusing on connection as your inspiration is that it may bring you in contact with other artists and aspiring creatives with whom you can continue to share work and inspiration. When teaching kids in rural Arkansas, Kuo would assign "I Am" poems, which consist of lines starting with "I am...."[66] "I had asked the students to tape their 'I Am' poems on the walls, to make them proud of their own writing. Then I noticed something surprising: They wanted to read one another's work. Certain students—who, during my attempts at collective reading, put their heads down or slapped the head of a studious classmate, trying to keep him from 'being good,' as they called it—would now stand attentively in front of a classmate's poem, tracing the line methodically with an index finger, not saying a word."

8.7 *Find New References*

French Impressionist Edgar Degas once said to poet Stéphane Mallarmé that he had a great idea for a poem. "But Degas," replied Mallarmé,[67] "You can't make a poem with ideas. ... You make it with words."

Words are one fundamental element of poetry and prose, and every form of creative work has its own.$^{\S6.1}$ This prompt is about identifying or referencing an example, sample, or inspiration you're not as familiar with, and applying it to your work. These examples are often called references—exemplary work that you can refer to as inspiration for your work.

---

66. https://theamericanscholar.org/reading-with-patrick/
67. https://en.wikiquote.org/wiki/St%C3%A9phane_Mallarm%C3%A9

If I'm looking for new elements to reference as an author, I would be looking for new words in the dictionary, or finding new sentence structures I could try.

If you work in film or the recording arts, sounds, scenes, and storyboards are references as well. Filmmaker David Lynch calls this "firewood," and is constantly looking out for and stockpiling music to inspire his scenes in his films.

You can find references across different crafts. For example, filmmaker Paul Thomas Anderson was struggling with a script about two fighting families, when he came across Upton Sinclair's *Oil!* Anderson says,[68] "When I read the book there were so many ready-made scenes, and the great venue of the oil fields and all that. Those were kind of the obvious things that seemed worth making a film about." When Anderson stumbled across that reference, he was able to unblock his script which became the film *There Will be Blood*. The story itself deviated too far from *Oil!* to be called an adaptation, though its inspirations are clearly in the throughline of the film.[§13.2]

As you get familiar with the tools and techniques available, if you're lucky, you might even cobble something together that no one else has tried or imagined. This is how originality *actually* works: not through a mythological lightning bolt of insight, but through constant bricolage, rediscovery, and remixing of references.

8.8 *Pick a Neglected Idea*

Instead of shelving an idea,[§12.7] pick an idea you've put on a shelf—or simply neglected—and develop it. Write down three ways you can change the idea to make it meet your quality criteria.[§9]

In *Walk Through Walls*, performance artist Marina Abramović writes of an exercise where she gives her students a thousand pieces of white paper. The students write down ideas. They keep the ones they like, and trash the ones they don't. After three months, Abramović only takes ideas from the trash cans; she calls these the "treasure trove" of the things her students are afraid to do.

---

68. http://www.blackfilm.com/20071221/features/danieldaylewis.shtml

Remember, each idea holds potential to be the one that changes your life. If you revisit an idea and have the sense that it's special, don't be afraid to commit to it.

↤ **Or flip this prompt:** *Archive an Idea*§12.7

9 Decide What Quality Means

"Ease isn't the goal; excellence is."

— Ed Catmull

There's a difference between what you think quality and progress mean and how other people receive your work. You have to define what quality means.

Patagonia founder Yvon Chouinard, who writes in *Let My People Go Surfing*, "Striving to make the best *quality* product is the reason we got into business in the first place." Patagonia's definition of quality involves invention, global design, ease of care and cleaning, added value, authenticity, beauty, and the core customer's needs.

Pixar's former chief creative officer John Lasseter says, "Quality is the best business plan." In his book *Creativity Inc.*, Pixar co-founder Ed Catmull talks about the company's definition of quality as one that highly values people—finding, developing, and supporting good people, who "in turn will find, develop, and own good ideas."

In an ideal world, everybody wants to make something that other people admire and love. (And, hopefully, pay for.) For many of us, that's inherent to the definition of quality. But as actor Ethan Hawke says,[69] that definition of quality is actually the enemy: "Because it's not up to us whether what we do is any good. And if history has taught us anything, the world is an extremely unreliable critic."

This chapter sets out to support you to define quality beyond just something good and admirable to other people, and creating your own definition of it. "The definition of quality in the creator's mind is the one that's ever changing," says Chris Kim. "Whatever quality means to you, that's what ultimately defines who you are as a creative."

9.1 *Form an Opinion*

In 2007, Ye (then known as Kanye West) founded and ran the blog called UniverseCity. The blog became well known as a source of inspiration, connecting the worlds of art and architecture with mainstream pop culture. The *New York Times* called it "a masterpiece blog."[70]

West ran UniverseCity with the help of a small team, including graphic designer Joe Perez. Perez was responsible for supplying and researching the content, making ideas available to West to curate, comment on, and approve. Even though Perez had formally studied at the Art Center College of Design,[71] he has likened research for the blog to returning to art school—and studying every major simultaneously. "You can say you do research every day, but when something forces you to look at thousands of images on a daily basis, the best of the best, it starts to definitely have an impact on you on a really basic level," he says. This exposure to a vast quantity of images seems to have remained with West, who would report looking at 800 images a day[72] several years after the blog ended.

Part of what Perez brought to the table was geographic; he had access to the Rhode Island School of Design library, where he discovered inspiration and references in books that weren't as easily found on the internet. But looking at thousands of images wasn't the only thing that refined Joe's

69. https://www.youtube.com/watch?v=WRS9Gek4V5Q

70. https://www.nytimes.com/2008/08/10/magazine/10wwln-medium-t.html

71. https://www.youtube.com/watch?v=nX6p7ZQT4c8

72. https://www.youtube.com/watch?v=-ErEZvuWoVs

taste. There was also the thought process and dialogue that he and West developed to select and curate images for UniverseCity. Managing the blog required that both of them develop and refine opinions on the mountains of images that Perez selected.

Understand that while uninformed opinions are common, informed opinions are rare, interesting, and actually useful. Put in the work to develop and discover your opinions. Through rigorous and consistent studying, you'll realize what your sensibilities and values are. Know the other possibilities, perhaps even better than the people who support them know it.

It's these attempts and documentation that will serve you amidst difficult times. Understanding quality is not difficult; it starts as you immerse yourself in a lot of really good work and develop your own opinions on them. You won't do good work until you define what good means to you.

9.2 *Create a Quality Rubric*

I've developed a definition of quality for all kinds of work I create. When assessing the quality of an article idea, for example, I look at timing, societal impact, counterintuition, action steps, and prior coverage. I discovered these attributes through noticing what ideas were accepted and rejected, through patterns I noticed in what I liked to read, and through papers I read. I refine the meaning of these words often, based on feedback from editors.

Criteria can be fluid; for me, they're almost like rubrics, where I consider each of these factors, and I write down guiding questions to help me evaluate or test an idea. They also help me formulate the idea and position it.

For example, if I was looking at prior coverage, I would want to figure out how often this idea has been written about before, and in what ways. Do I have anything new to offer? Can I connect the big idea with a different small event, that's more timely and relevant? Or is there an event that I can connect with a new idea?

I often write these questions down in second person, as if a writing coach were sending them to me. When I review each piece before I've decided that it's done, I often also go through each of the criteria to make sure I can check it off.

As you develop your capabilities and perspective, you may find that list of questions getting longer. For example, in *Let My People Go Surfing*, Patagonia founder Yvon Chouinard writes of his own list of criteria to evaluate potential product ideas: Is it functional? Multifunctional? Is it durable? Does it fit our customer? Will people be able to repair it? Is the product and line simple? Is it an innovation or invention? Is it a global design? Is it easy to care for and clean? Does it have any added value? Is it authentic? Is it beautiful? Are we just chasing fashion? Are we designing for our core customer?

As a starting point, choose a creator in your field that you admire. Learn more about their process, through their own memoirs and interviews, or through other people analyzing their work. Be mindful of the standards that start jumping out at you.

You might also see whether the creatives you admire have written about their own quality criteria, as many have: The 20th century poet W.H. Auden put out his criteria for major poets,[73] Robert Caro shows some of his thought process in his book *Working*, and Mary Robinette provides feedback for editing articles.[74] If you want to emulate author, programmer, and entrepreneur Derek Sivers, he shows you how.[75] The same with Y Combinator founder Paul Graham.[76] You could also study any other writing you like, and learn how you can improve.[77]

Practically speaking, I've found that the best time to strictly apply these standards of quality is in the verification stage of the creative process. I'm interested in completing the idea and making sure it's polished enough for me to be satisfied with. However, I deliberately do not apply these standards to my generative work, like writing in a journal or notebook, if I'm just taking a note,[78] or writing a blog post for fun. At those stages, I'm still exploring and discovering what I have to say on a topic. The idea is too fragile to go through this process. It still needs to be nurtured and developed.

---

73. https://www.theatlantic.com/past/docs/issues/67oct/davison.htm
74. https://twitter.com/nbashaw/status/1237131727635501056
75. https://sivers.org/
76. http://www.paulgraham.com/useful.html
77. https://medium.com/swlh/
    5-techniques-to-learn-anything-with-or-without-anyones-help-1f7bcea9ee2a
78. https://herbertlui.net/8-lessons-from-800-note-cards-in-the-zettelkasten/

9.3 *Define Acceptable*

Once you've defined what quality means to you, you can also define what is acceptable: the minimum bar for quality, a passable mark. Not complete, certainly not perfect, but *acceptable* for you to declare that it's done.

When you choose to make something acceptable, rather than perfect, you reduce the expectations and ensuing pressure that could block your creativity. You complete your work,[79] stay motivated, knowing another opportunity is just around the corner, which provides another chance to make something interesting.[80]

Knowing what acceptable means to you helps when you're deciding whether or not a creative work—or a version of it—is actually done. You might double check to see if all the parts of your work pass your standard. In my line of work (writing) that means I'll edit my draft three times before it's done. I check it for grammar, voice, tone, and flow. Similar to a factory line, though, it's best to also add in other stages to check the work's quality, so there aren't any unpleasant surprises at the end.

This can literally be a series of sentences that enable you to communicate when something is done. For example, the GitHub team published the philosophies that drove their decision making in a document known as The Zen of GitHub, which includes this quality check:[81] "It's not fully shipped until it's fast." If you want to declare something as fully complete at GitHub, you need to make it fast, probably meeting a maximum of some predefined set of milliseconds.

As I heard from recording artist and amateur bodybuilder Kim Jong-kook, the workout doesn't end at the gym: "You're only done after you eat." He said,[82] "Some people don't eat after working out to lose weight. You have to eat to build muscle. If you don't eat, it's just labor." In other words, if you want to declare your workout acceptable, you need to be as mindful of how you nourish your body—with the quantities and types of macronutrients you need—as you are of what exercises you do.

For me, I check if my idea is acceptable as a pitch, before I even write it up. Pitches for my articles are acceptable when I've explained to myself

---

79. https://www.researchgate.net/publication/232418484_Improving_Students'_Perceptions_of_ a_Mathematics_Assignment_by_Increasing_Problem_Completion_Rates_Is_Problem_ Completion_a_Reinforcing_Event
80. https://hbr.org/2011/05/the-power-of-small-wins
81. https://ben.balter.com/2015/08/12/the-zen-of-github/
82. https://www.youtube.com/watch?v=pPSSHGvFFR8

and the reader why the idea is well timed, what it means to society, what people may misunderstand about it, what people can take away from this story and apply to their lives, and how few people have covered it before. If the pitch fails in some way (for example, if a lot of people have covered it before), the pitch does not pass, and it is not acceptable. I'm happy, as I didn't need to spend time writing the entire story out only to realize this—I didn't try to make it perfect before I made it acceptable.

9.4 *Visit the Greats*

"If you have writer's block, you're not reading enough," says poet Nikki Giovanni to author Mason Currey.[83] In order to improve your output, you first need to improve your input. Experiencing other people's work is the best first step to understanding what quality might even mean in your field. Everyone who is making something, right now, has been inspired by someone else.

I'm personally not a huge fan of lists. But, if you don't have any references or places in mind, start with the greatest-of-all-time lists for your field. For example, if you're making music, you could look at Mojo's Top 100 albums of all time, or perhaps just of the last decade. If you have no idea where to start, look for your favorites in the list, or start at the top and work your way down.

Pay attention to what you notice. Dacoury Natche first notices the beat on a song, not the lyrics. Michael Saviello steps right up to the painting and starts looking at it. Don't worry too much about what to do. Just try, and you'll know.

Besides making time to experience art, look into the lives of artists. Dive into their creative processes and their perspectives on their craft. Read their biographies. Study their heroes, too. Know the bar that your heroes set for themselves, and set your own in that direction as well.

Eventually, it's also important for you to experience work outside of your field. For example, a person who writes can find inspiration in a song, or a coder might be inspired by a design. But this prompt suggests first understanding what excellence means and feels like in your field.

---

83. https://subtlemaneuvers.substack.com/p/robert-lowell-kept-a-double-bed-in

9.5 *Study the Craft*

Select a piece of work you love or that is revered in your field. Study it. Answer this question: "What makes it great?"

Write down the first thing that stands out to you about the piece of work. Then, write down the second thing. And the third thing, and so on, until you don't notice any more unique things. Then, read someone else's commentary on the work—or if none exists, just call a friend and ask them what they notice about the piece. What do they experience that you didn't? What interests them? What's the difference between what you noticed and what they noticed?

For example, if you're a writer studying an article you really like, write down the first 20 lines that interest you, and compare them with the first 20 lines of the piece. Or compare your 20 lines with 20 lines that another writer identifies, or perhaps 20 lines that an editor identifies.

In software, there's a method of testing called rubber duck debugging.[84] The method is simple—you explain to a rubber duck what your code is supposed to do and talk it out line by line. You can tell it what you plan on doing next as well. The rubber duck, in this case, doesn't need to be for debugging; it can be the listener to your experience of a piece of art. If you're shy and don't want to explain yourself to a friend yet, try it with a rubber duck.

These are all actions you can take to *pay attention*. Focus on the work. Watch how you react to it. Don't blind yourself with the craftsperson or artist's reputation. Instead, use other people's reactions or reviews of the work as windows into your own—not as your own talking points. Understand why other people consider the work great, and, most importantly, decide whether you agree, and why.

9.6 *Copy a Classic*

Michelangelo was a highly-skilled forger,[85] and selling a counterfeit sculpture would actually impress the buyer and earn him his first patron.[86] Vin-

---

84. https://rubberduckdebugging.com/

85. https://www.npr.org/2015/06/23/412244490/
could-the-masterpiece-be-a-fake-profit-revenge-and-the-art-of-forgery

86. https://www.artsy.net/article/
artsy-editorial-how-michelangelo-got-his-start-by-forging-antiquities

cent van Gogh copied Hiroshige, Paul Gauguin copied Édouard Manet, Paul Cézanne the Old Masters. Ye (the artist formerly known as Kanye West) re-created many hip-hop songs from the 90s[87] to teach himself how to produce music.

Figure: "Flowering plum tree, after Hiroshige" by Vincent van Gogh, 1887. Credit: Niels,[88] Wikimedia Commons.[89]

---

87. https://www.youtube.com/watch?v=zrpMihSD3uI

88. https://www.flickr.com/people/73536601@N00

89. https://commons.wikimedia.org/wiki/File:WLANL_-_Pachango_-_De_bloeiende_ pruimenboom_(Naar_Hiroshige),_Vincent_van_Gogh_(1887).jpg

Figure: Woodblock print of "Plum garden at Kameido" by Utagawa Hiroshige, 1857. Credit: Chester Beatty Library and Wikimedia Commons.[90]

While most people might use the words *imitating* and *copying* interchangeably, there is a subtle and important difference. To imitate is to represent, reinterpret, or reproduce the style and vision of someone else's work. To copy is to try to make an exact duplicate.

---

90. https://commons.wikimedia.org/wiki/File:Plum_garden_at_Kameido_(Kameido_umeyashiki)_(
    CBL_J_2693).jpg

The goal of this prompt is to get you thinking about and feeling what it's like to make something that you appreciate. Of course, this isn't the final goal of your creative work; it's an exercise to improve your skills. Hunter S. Thompson typed out *The Great Gatsby* just to get the feeling of what it was like to write that way.[91] The idea of "copywork" has been applied to UI design[92] and software development,[93] too. If I'm typing the same words someone else wrote, I can't claim originality over it, but it is a learning exercise.

You might find yourself facing gaps in your own skill and knowledge. It's in copying that we experience a new dimension of the work—at the very least, a similar technical problem-solving that the original artist had experienced as well.

9.7 *Imitate a Classic*

To imitate is to represent, reinterpret, or reproduce the style and vision of someone else's work. To copy[§9.6] is to try to make an exact duplicate. Imitation is not superior to copying—both have their place. You might need to imitate before you know how to copy exactly. For example, if you were to re-create a song you really liked, you might need to find the right instrument, drumkit, or sound file, and figure out what the layers sound like. But to imitate, you find your own way to recreate the original.

When I asked Dacoury Natche how he learned to make music, he spoke of imitating as a way to refine his own technique as he was first getting started. There will be things that you don't know how to do yet, and that's the point. When you don't know something, do whatever you can to replicate it. As producer Chris Kim pointed out, the search for the answer and attempts to imitate or reproduce the original often provide more interesting results than recreating the original idea in the precise steps of the original creator.

---

91. https://www.newyorker.com/magazine/2005/03/07/believer

92. https://www.smashingmagazine.com/2017/02/improving-ui-design-skills-copywork/

93. https://daveceddia.com/learn-react-with-copywork/

9.8 *Remix a Piece*

When Dacoury Natche and I met, Kazakh music producer Imanbek's remix of SAINt JHN's "Roses" was at the top of our charts. I was on a road trip a few days prior and heard it at least twice an hour.

While the original artist SAINt JHN released "Roses" three years prior, it was the remix that was picked up on social media and broke through to mainstream radio stations, bringing the original with it. Essentially, the original served as a demo for a much more popular remix.

Remixing is at the heart of popular music. DJ Kool Herc sampled the best part of songs and hip-hop emerged as an art form. Hip-hop is one of the best examples of creativity involving mainly combining ideas. As Maria Popova writes in *The Marginalian*,[94] "I frequently use LEGO as a metaphor for combinatorial creativity—if we only have bricks of one shape, size, and color, what we build with them remains limited; but if we build with pieces of various shapes, sizes, and colors, our creations will be infinitely more interesting."

And before all of that, there was shanzhai (山寨). Before DJ Kool Herc, or combinatorial creativity emerged as a key component to creative work, there was shanzhai. While the term shanzhai is usually used today to describe counterfeit products[95] (think of fake Nokia phones, the Motoloba,[96] or Harry Potter and the Porcelain Doll[97]), the word is built on a philosophy of creativity, "The Chinese idea of the original is determined not by a unique act of creation, but by unending process, not by definitive identity but by constant change."

Byung-Chul Han writes that while a shanzhai product might be considered fake, that doesn't mean they are inferior: "The ingenuity of shanzhai products is frequently superior to that of the original. For example, one shanzhai cell phone has the additional function of being able to identify counterfeit money. In this way it has established itself as an original. The new emerges from surprising variations and combinations."[98]

---

94. https://www.themarginalian.org/2012/06/01/the-art-of-scientific-investigation-beveridge-2/

95. https://www.wsj.com/articles/SB123257138952903561

96. https://web.archive.org/web/20110714145919/http://techrice.com/2011/06/20/shanzhai-factory-life-the-making-of-a-motoloba/

97. https://www.nytimes.com/2007/08/10/opinion/10potter2.html

98. Han, Byung-Chul. *Shanzhai: Deconstruction in Chinese*. Translated by Philippa Hurd. The MIT Press, 2017.

In this prompt, you will be tapping into this idea of unending process by making a remix[§9.8] of your own work. Select one of the ideas you've completed. It could be your favorite idea or your least favorite idea. It could be the most popular one or the least popular one. You can ask your friend to choose from a bunch of options, or just randomly select one. Just pick one. After you've picked one, duplicate it (digitally or physically), and modify it by at least 3%, the percentage by which designer Virgil Abloh modified an original piece of work.[99]

For a song, that might just mean tweaking a small portion of its running time, or supplementing it throughout with an infrequent chord or pattern. For a video, it might mean moving segments around or adding in a short new scene. For a painting, it might mean adding a new layer of paint somewhere—covering a figure, or creating a new one, or just adding to the background. Choose a part to change and a way to change it. (You can choose to modify by more than 3%, but give yourself some constraint.[§7])

Similarly, you could choose to remix through reduction. Author and Princeton instructor John McPhee writes about a technique called "greening"—to "green" an opening paragraph by three means to cut three lines out of the paragraph as a way of forcing the editing process. He writes,[100] "Green 4 does not mean lop off four lines at the bottom. ... The idea is to remove words in such a manner that no one would notice that anything has been removed."

Remixing may become part of your draft, demo, and sketch[§5.4] process. For example, for three months, seven days a week, 16 hours per day, graphic designer Joe Perez worked on Kanye West's *Cruel Summer* album cover. In a video Perez uploaded on YouTube,[101] there are 325 different variations of the album cover.

When you decide that your remix has become a draft of its own, save it as a new piece of work with a different title.

---

99. https://hypebeast.com/2018/6/virgil-abloh-interview-hypebeast-magazine

100. https://www.newyorker.com/magazine/2015/09/14/omission

101. https://www.youtube.com/watch?v=IwJoYPyzlw4

9.9 *Obsess over Details*

Obsession is one of the core aspects of craftsmanship. Detail, perfection, and progression are all fruits of obsession, an absolutist view on the correctness, integrity, or honesty of something. These traits often provide a breeding ground for great work.

"The details are not details—they make the product just like details make the architecture. The gauge of the wire, the selection of the wood, the finish of the castings—the connections, the connections, the connections," writes designer and architect Charles Eames.[102] You could also make the case that a creative work is nothing more than a sum of details.

Author Robert Caro writes of his obsession with research in *Working*: "Whatever it is that makes me do research the way I do, it's not something I'm proud of, and it's not something for which I can take the credit—or the blame. It just seems to be a part of me."

We, too, must cultivate an obsession with our work. For me, in my writing, it's about rigorous fact-checking and correctness. It's about speaking in my voice, and doing the work it takes to figure out what that even means. Sometimes, it's merely about a headline or, more likely, a lede—where I constantly tweak it to try to make it better. Other times, it's about finding a fact or verifying an apocryphal tale to support a point.

To practice your detail-orientation, try choosing one thing to focus on for thirty minutes.

Zooming in on a small part of your work is a great interpretation of this prompt. You could focus your attention on one particular corner, or a 1-inch by 1-inch, area of your artwork. Or, if you're making a song, focus on nailing the lyrics in the opening verse, or the harmonies on the bridge.

---

102. https://twitter.com/eamesoffice/status/1233482403336814593?lang=bg

In music or computer hardware, you could also choose to focus on the time, pace, and tempo of your work. The thing you choose to obsess over might never be noticed outright by your viewers, readers, or audience—but *you* will know. For example, Apple made[103] the blinking light sleep indicators on its laptops mimic the average number of breaths a person takes. You probably never knew that, but the creators knew it would make a difference in the quality of what they made.

Obsession can create the energy that takes your work to the next level.

↪ **Or flip this prompt:** *Stop Obsessing*[§12.1]

---

103. https://patents.google.com/patent/US6658577B2/en

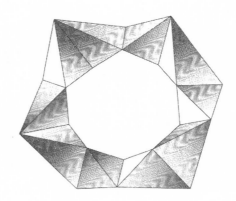

10 Communicate Your Work

*"As long as you're comfortable walking your truth, no one will
ever beat you at being you, either."*

— Curtis "50 Cent" Jackson

When you visit a museum or gallery, you'll notice that each piece of art is usually accompanied by an artist statement. Each art show is accompanied by ephemera like brochures, as well as an audio guide. Curators know even the most accessible artwork can't speak for itself to everyone; they need to provide context.

You may encounter a similar experience at a restaurant: a staff member presents the food, explaining the story behind a recipe, or where a key ingredient was sourced. The restaurant might even open up the kitchen, making every operation visible.

We see more value in things that were created through some effort, evidence that the creator really cares. When we show our process to people, we give them a chance to appreciate the work more, and to establish the value of the work we're presenting.

Here are some prompts you can accept, modify, or reject, to start to establish your work's value.

10.1 *Create Your Own Market*

When Vincent van Gogh died, he was not a well-known artist. His brother, Theo van Gogh, died six months later, leaving his widow, Johanna van Gogh-Bonger, the mission of promoting her brother-in-law's work. She inherited 200 of van Gogh's paintings,[104] which were worth so little at the time that she was advised to get rid of them. Perhaps Van Gogh-Bonger's mission was as much fueled by love and duty as it was an understanding of the work's potential. Although the general public didn't appreciate it yet, many artists admired Van Gogh's work but didn't have the money to pay for it.

Van Gogh-Bonger started a boarding house in Bussum, then a small village 15 miles from Amsterdam. She would meet people and form working relationships with them. She worked tirelessly with dealers, galleries, and museums, embedding herself in the art world. The work paid off and Van Gogh-Bonger coordinated 20 exhibits of Van Gogh's work in a decade. She also published her collection of letters between the Van Gogh brothers, which added to Vincent's reputation and drove up the value of his work. Eventually, she successfully placed his work in museums, and the market had gained the initial momentum it needed.

Some markets seem to emerge naturally, but others are made. In this case, Van Gogh-Bonger dedicated a significant part of her life to making a market for Vincent van Gogh's work. Even though Van Gogh's work was already complete, the reputation, awareness, and value of it weren't set in stone yet. Vincent van Gogh wasn't recognized as an artist until after he died, when his sister-in-law Johanna van Gogh-Bonger did the hard work of communicating and promoting Van Gogh's genius.

In an interview with the writer and designer Debbie Millman, artist Shantell Martin says,[105] "Create your own opportunities and do that by using what you have access to." She recalls her journey, moving away from a fanbase, contacts, and early success in Japan to continue her art career in New York City. She practically started from scratch, sleeping on friends'

---

104. http://www.webexhibits.org/vangogh/memoir/nephew/2.html

105. https://d.rip/debbie-millman/posts/design-matters-with-shantell-martin-xWKK3.html

couches and meeting new people, in a city abundant with competition. It seemed like everyone else was also an artist.

Without anyone offering her an opportunity, Martin would grow stagnant; so she decided to create her own. Borrowing her friend's space, she returned to an art form she used in Japan, but wasn't in demand in New York—projection and VJing. She invited her friends, who invited their friends, and so on. She recalls, "Eventually, someone sees it and says, 'Hey. I work for MoMA. Would love to do that at our friends and family event. And we're going to pay you to do that.'"

Martin elaborated in an interview with me for this book: "Now more than ever, I like to tell younger artists that it's really important to turn your weaknesses into your strengths. If you're not comfortable hosting shows or parties, find a collaborator to help you in that area but force yourself to do it little by little until it's [something that you're comfortable with].

"It's not really about being a promoter, but doing what you can to put yourself and your work out into the world in a way that is also still authentic to who you are and the work you want to make."

You can share your work in all sorts of ways. You can share it on social media, you can send out monthly email updates to friends, you can host a listening party$^{§11.5}$ for your new song collection.

Value is a very amorphous concept, and yet we all know a form of value when we experience it. Service is a form of value. Usefulness. Education. Experience. Excitement. Entertainment. Symbolism.

Your work is already valuable in its own way. These series of prompts are designed to support you to get other people to see what you see. You don't need to want to be the next Vincent van Gogh to communicate the value of your work. You might find them useful to simply start conversations with your audience, customers, collectors, and handlers. If you're interested in becoming a working creator or artist, these prompts will get you started, and I suggest checking out Michael Ardelean's *Art for Money*,[106] another Holloway book, which is totally dedicated to getting paid what you deserve for what you create.

There might not even be a commercial motive. Maybe you simply want friends and family to understand you and your work better. Or maybe you're interested in working together with another creator and want to start the collaboration well. In both of these cases, communicating the

106. https://www.holloway.com/b/art-for-money

value and intention of the work is crucial to getting the creative process started.

Here are some prompts you can accept, modify, or reject, to start to establish your work's value.

10.2 *Set up Surfaces*

It's tempting to see your work as either complete or incomplete. Perfect or crap. But there are many different stages of your work and, accordingly, many virtual and physical places you can store your work. This is essential to taking action and releasing work regularly. You'll need to prepare spaces to incubate the work you don't feel so good about, the work that hasn't reached a stage that you can call acceptable.[§9.3]

A surface can be any place you're performing or storing your work. One surface could be private, like a folder or a box that no one else will see.[§11.3] Another surface could be semi-public, one that you show to people you trust. Still, another surface could be entirely public, ready to show the world.

Set up at least three different surfaces—one for storing your works in progress, one for sending to other people for feedback, and one for displaying your finished work. You can choose how visible each surface is. You can set up more, if you like. Vin Verma started his own surface, which he calls Futureland,[107] to track his daily routines and creative activities. He has grown it into a network of digital journals, where people can either publicly or privately track their own progress on their projects.

10.3 *Take Someone Behind the Scenes*

One of the simplest ways of communicating value is showing the effort that actually went into the work. That might involve literally showing the process of making it, though it might also be more biographical. You may ask yourself, and answer, questions like:

- When did you first get the idea for this piece of work?
- How did the idea start?

---

107. https://futureland.tv/

- What did you see throughout this process?
- Who influenced the work?
- What parts of the work might have emerged from stories in your life?
- What skills did creating this work require? If you had these skills already, how did you hone them? If you didn't, how did you learn them or who did you work with?
- How many times did you try making this work?

This process involves metacognition—thinking about how you think. If you find it too heavy a lift on your own, you can act as if you're talking to your best friend about it. You could also enlist the help of a friend who might be available.

When you start to answer these questions, you're taking someone behind the scenes of your work. You're also learning to articulate the value of the work, based on what went into it. (To borrow an industrial analogy, this would be describing the raw material and the processing.) You could write it all up, or record a video, or prepare this communication in whichever media you feel most comfortable with.

When Michael Saviello talks about his work, he also offers to show it to the person he's talking to. He allows them enough space and time to take it in, and he can see how they're processing it. He doesn't just plunk them down; he learns about the person. Sometimes, he even lets them sit in, watch him paint, and ask questions along the way.

↔ **Or flip this prompt:** *Make Something You Won't Ever Show Anyone Else*[§11.3]

10.4 *Make Them Curious*

If people had the attention span to sit for a few hours with your work, then certainly it would speak for itself. But, they don't. Still, if they were curious to learn more, or knew how to help you, they would. If you experience a reluctance, hesitation, or fear of telling people about your work, it's even a greater reason to try. The more reluctant you are to talk about your work, the more potential you're blocking up.

Derek Sivers writes in *Your Music, Your People*, that when people ask you about your work, giving a boring answer is rude. I wouldn't go that far, though I would agree that even just a minute of preparation could help. Sivers writes, "Before the conference, come up with one interesting sentence that says what you do—including a curious bit that will make them ask a follow-up question." He gives the example of, instead of saying "I'm a bassist," introducing yourself as "Bassist of the Crunchy Frogs—the worst punk bluegrass band ever. We're headlining the showcase tonight. Our singer is a pirate."

If I were talking about my book, for example, I wouldn't say, "I'm an author," I'd say something like, "I'm the author of *Creative Doing*, a book that debunks the biggest lie in creative thinking. It has 75 prompts to make the reader more creative. It's the only book with a shape as a mascot."

↬ **Or flip this prompt:** *Lose Yourself*§6.5

10.5 *Sell Out*

> *"Some people are like, 'Oh, yeah, just sell out and do pop music.'*
> *So you !@#$ing do it, then! It's not easy."*
> — Abel Tesfaye, The Weeknd[108]

When Will Smith decided he wanted to become the biggest movie star in the world, he worked with his business partner James Lassiter to examine a list of the ten top-grossing movies of all time. In his memoir *Will*, he writes, "It was crystal clear: Ten out of the top ten films of all time had special effects. Nine out of ten had special effects and creatures. Eight out of ten had special effects, creatures, and a romantic storyline. (We would ultimately discover that all of the top ten movies were about love, but we didn't notice that back then.)"

When Smith was approached with a $10 million offer to star in *8 Heads in a Duffel Bag*, the analysis made it clearer that Lassiter and Smith should say no. And when Smith was approached to appear in *Six Degrees of Separation*, he and Lassiter said yes to a much smaller offer of $300,000—and set the foundation for Smith's career as a movie star.

In this prompt, take something popular, identify elements and patterns, and infuse them into your own work.

---

108. Eells, Josh. "Sex, Drugs and R&B: Inside the Weeknd's Dark Twisted Fantasy."[109] *Rolling Stone*, no. 1247, Oct. 2015.

109. https://www.rollingstone.com/music/music-news/
sex-drugs-and-rb-inside-the-weeknds-dark-twisted-fantasy-176091/

I've found the process of trying to make a hit—not always the end result—to be useful. If you're making music, you can immerse yourself in the top charts. If you're making visual art, you can see what work is going viral or is popular with collectors. If you're making digital products, check out what's resonating with charts like Product Hunt or the Apple App Store.

If you're a writer like me you might immerse yourself in the news cycle, or go look into the Popular or Trending feed, and just look at the things people are engaging with. I'll come up with 10 ideas[§8.1] myself, based on *those* ideas. Or, I'll just look into my own data and analytics, and find an idea that a lot of people are reading. Most of the time, I don't pick the ideas back up. But sometimes, I pick an idea and actually double down on it. I test it to see if a lot of people might actually like it.

If you experience a strong aversion to this prompt, know that it might involve the crummiest, hackiest, of all verbs: Pander. Copy. Steal. Make something kitschy. Make your worst piece of work—the one that the popular creatives, whom you don't necessarily admire, do.

It's not "selling out" unless you make money from it—you can go through this process and not release anything, especially if you feel it compromises your standard of quality. But the goal here is to meet people where they are, and to develop the makings of an understanding of what works.

At the end of it, once you're done with your idea, if you feel like it's a commodity or repetitive, that's the way it should be. But if you're happy with your idea, then you could consider finding a surface to display it on,[§10.2] or a person to show it to. After all, you may have met the world halfway and just come up with a breakthrough idea.

➡ **Or flip this prompt:** *Set a Mission*[§13.2]

11 Get Feedback

While our earliest steps might involve making things for ourselves, we also must eventually show someone else our work. The goal isn't validation, recognition, or business. Rather, the fact that we know someone else will experience it will enable us to figure out and further refine what we're trying to say.

It's almost as if there's a compulsion inside us—perhaps personified by the judge[§5.6]—that really wakes up when we know that somebody else is watching. This compulsion will enable us to take our work to the next level.

11.1 *Experiment Your Way to Something Big*

> "*Science for me is very close to art. ... Scientific discovery is an irrational act. It's an intuition which turns out to be reality at the end of it—and I see no difference between a scientist*

*developing a marvelous discovery and an artist making a
painting."*

— Carlo Rubbia[110]

In 2014, while she was working at Google, Sarah Cooper found an old note. Years earlier, she had seen a colleague make a strong impression in a meeting with a completely nonsensical Venn diagram. She wrote down "How to look smart in a meeting," with a note to herself to draw Venn diagrams. She added another nine parodical observations, and published her first post on Medium. She said,[111] "It was just really—to use the cliché, it was low-hanging fruit for me to be able to finish it, especially since I was in a ton of meetings at the time anyway."

Cooper eventually migrated these blog posts to her own parody blog, titled *The Cooper Review*. A year prior, she'd started a parody of *Cosmopolitan*, called *oolalove!*,[112] and made videos on YouTube. She illustrated by tracing photos she took of her friends. She made a calendar. For a short while, she even made memes.[113] Millions of people read her work at Medium and *The Cooper Review*, leading her to a three-book deal.

Cooper's willingness to try new things and see how they work out is crucial to her success. So is feedback.

Before Cooper publishes any work, she shares her ideas with a small group of friends and family. "I look for a few different kinds of feedback. Sometimes I'm just like, 'Oh, I have this idea, what do you think?' or, 'I have this idea, let me know if you have any other ideas,' or something like that. And I'm looking for if people think it's funny at all, even if they don't have anything to contribute, I still want to know if the idea is a funny idea. Some people just like the post or laugh at it or they'll contribute ideas.

"It's turned out to be a pretty good gauge of how well something will do, 'cause sometimes I'll put something out there and people don't really like it on my private page, but I'll go ahead with it anyway just because I like it. But even in those situations, the response I get in the private group is pretty indicative of the response I'm going to get publicly."

110. Wolpert, Lewis, Alison Richards. *Passionate Minds: The Inner World of Scientists.* Oxford University Press, 1997, p. 197.

111. https://www.huffpost.com/entry/how-this-ex-googler-got-a-book-deal-writing-about-meetings_b_58f54d98e4b04cae050dca2c

112. https://web.archive.org/web/20131227051924/http://oolalove.com/

113. https://medium.com/more-or-less/facebook-zombies-f8a690084c0d

The problem has two parts. First, each of us has limited time and energy—we can't do *everything* we want to do. Second, it would be nice if we could always forecast what resonates with people and what won't, but nobody can. Cooper solved this by running small experiments with her friends and family, and seeing what people responded to.

Cooper continued moving forward with her work, trying new things, until another small bet paid huge results years later. This time, Cooper tried TikTok. Her first video had the caption "How to emote with your eyes when you're wearing a mask." In the next ones, she mimicked some of Donald Trump's speeches, both lip-syncing and speaking in her voice with his mannerisms. She also lip-synced Poppy Jennings and filmed a walk with her dog.

Perhaps it was because of her instinct, paired up with the feedback and data, that Cooper decided to double down on the Donald Trump lip syncs, each of which went viral. She grew her audiences on TikTok and Twitter, with many—including prominent people in the entertainment industry—showing public appreciation for her work. In the following months, Cooper would guest host for Jimmy Fallon, and sign deals with Netflix and CBS.

If you ever find that imposter syndrome blocks you from talking about your work or asking for feedback, consider legendary comedian, actress, and writer Tina Fey's words,[114] "The beauty of the impostor syndrome is you vacillate between extreme egomania, and a complete feeling of: 'I'm a fraud! Oh god, they're on to me! I'm a fraud!' So you just try to ride the egomania when it comes and enjoy it, and then slide through the idea of fraud. Seriously, I've just realized that almost everyone is a fraud, so I try not to feel too bad about it."

Here are some prompts to get you started with seeking feedback:

11.2 *Release Your Work*

When you release your work, you show the world—and yourself—that you are worth the space. You declare it. You get used to sharing your work, even if it's not your best, or if it's not perfect. You tell yourself, as Lindsay Jean Thomson said, "I have a right to be here. I have a right to cre-

---

114. https://www.independent.co.uk/arts-entertainment/films/features/
     tina-fey-from-spoofer-to-movie-stardom-1923552.html

ate. I have a right to be seen and appreciated." In addition to building your confidence, releasing your work can produce interesting tangible outcomes—whether it's new opportunities, feedback, or lessons you learn about yourself.

Now that you've put some work together, it's time for you to release something. Make it the main focus of your day. If you are releasing your work on a social network, just upload your work, release it, and then go on Airplane Mode. Do something else, so you're not worrying about how it performs.

It might feel natural for you to seek validation, especially early on if you're uncertain of your work, but the residue of the data will take up a lot of attention. And if it falls below your expectations, then the feedback (or lack thereof) might feel discouraging. It's more fruitful to spend the time enjoying yourself, at least.

I'd encourage you to reward yourself after you release your work, regardless of how other people receive it. If you're anything like me, releasing your work will be scary and involve checking your phone or computer a dozen times an hour to see if anyone liked it. This could put you into an unproductive headspace.[115] After all, we don't control how other people receive our work—only if and how we release it.

Consider actor and filmmaker Tommy Wiseau, who created and starred in the cult classic *The Room*. While he may have been making a genuine attempt to make a critically acclaimed film, it was not well received, or even taken seriously. Still, people loved it for different reasons. As actor and filmmaker James Franco puts it,[116] "*The Room* is not the worst movie. It is the *best* worst movie." And in an unpredictable outcome, Wiseau ended up making his living as a filmmaker. There was also the notorious creative process of filming *The Room*, which Greg Sestero and Tom Bissell document in the memoir *The Disaster Artist*. *The Disaster Artist* and *The Room* then served as Franco and Seth Rogen's own departure point[§5.5] for their film, titled after the memoir.

Imagine all of the other movies as badly made as *The Room* that we will never hear about. And yet, it worked. This is why creative work is, at best, probabilistic; there will always be outliers, and *The Room* is one of them. But that doesn't mean there isn't a principle to learn here: if Wiseau

115. https://www.sciencedirect.com/science/article/abs/pii/S0749597809000399
116. https://www.vanityfair.com/hollywood/2017/09/
    james-franco-the-room-tommy-wiseau-disaster-artist

hadn't made and released the movie, then he would have had a very different career arc. Ultimately, investing in, shooting, producing, releasing, promoting, and distributing *The Room* may have been the best decision he made for his creative work, and for the artists who were inspired by his story.

11.3 *Make Something You Won't Ever Show Anyone Else*

In *Minor Feelings*, poet Cathy Park Hong writes, "We say we don't care about audience, but it is a lie. Poets can be obsessed with status and are some of the most ingratiating people I know. ... A poet's precious avenue for mainstream success is through an award system dependent on the painstaking compromise of a jury panel, which can often guarantee that the anointed book will be free of aesthetic or political risk."

All too often, considering an audience gets in the way of creative work. It's not an easy habit or thought pattern to break; even if you think you're not making for an audience, you've gotten into the practice of it. The key is to practice making something you'll never show anyone else. In doing this, you're gaining valuable feedback from yourself.

One of Dacoury Natche's collaborators, Donald Glover (who makes music as Childish Gambino) has talked about the importance of making work that you won't show anyone else.[117] Glover says, "Making songs now that I know aren't going to be heard by anybody else, it is an interesting thing. Because I think you have to do that now as an artist. I really do. Because you start to manipulate your work based on other people, which is fine depending on what you're trying to do."

---

117. https://grantland.com/features/donald-glover-childish-gambino-grammys/

It's only once you've gotten in the groove of making things you won't show anyone else that you'll make something truer to what you want to make, that enables you to find the stories you want to tell, that are worth taking risks for, and eventually to find your creative purpose.

↤ Or flip this prompt: *Take Someone Behind the Scenes*$^{\S10.3}$

11.4 *Find New Contexts for Your Work*

I've been writing online for years. With the best of intentions, friends would suggest that I start a vlog, or a podcast. It used to bother me, but now I take it as part of a vast feedback channel. Instead of starting a vlog or podcast myself, I look for people who work in those areas and try to get my work out to them. Rather than repeating my work or reading it out loud, I prepare and improvise points from my writing into a more conversational format like an interview. I also keep my eyes open for visualizations that might better convey my message.

It's in making the work more portable that I'm able to put a portion of it out for feedback. The simplest version of this is getting feedback on names—which ones did a friend remember? Or, which concepts or ideas from an interview stood out to listeners or readers?

Chris Kim is obsessed with these different areas, which he calls contexts. It's important to him to find new contexts for his work. For example, he's interested in building in a more modular way—saving melodies in their own track, saving drums on another, and sharing these individual elements with people to get their perspectives.

Similarly, when Louis Vuitton menswear designer Virgil Abloh was working with his team on designs, he wouldn't be able to do it in person, so one of his team members would have to take photos or create digital versions so that everyone else could provide feedback through WhatsApp.[118] They transferred the item of clothing from the context of the physical world, into the context of an image on WhatsApp. When producing a song, you need to listen to the track in your car, through your headphones, and through all the speakers you can.

Context is not just about different media or forms, although that certainly counts. It might be the same piece of work but shared to a new audi-

---

118. https://www.instagram.com/p/CC8U17UFsN6/

ence (sharing a link or image of your work at a subreddit they're active in), or in a different place (I republish my article at *Forge* to *Business Insider*). Or, it might be taking that song you've produced and listening to it outside through a portable speaker or through your car stereo on a drive.

11.5 *Be Specific when Asking for Feedback*

When author Derek Sivers wrote every day for a month,[119] he realized that there wasn't enough time to take his writing to the standard he preferred and that he was emailing this subpar writing to tens of thousands of readers. He found it taxing to write something to his own standard every day, and he worried that he was emailing his audience too frequently. He stopped publishing every piece he wrote, only to release it publicly when ready.

You don't need to release your work to everyone for it to be complete. Sometimes, you might realize that a version of it is complete—but you're dissatisfied with it, or you want a second or third perspective on it. In situations like that, you can release it to a small group of friends or peers to get their feedback.

Asking for feedback on creative work is an incredibly difficult task. For starters, your family and friends will have an instinct to protect your feelings. Most acquaintances or strangers won't know you well enough to share. And how do you know what, and whom, to trust?

The first step is to clarify your intention when asking for feedback. You decide how to ask, whom to ask, and how you know whom to ask, when you decide what you're interested in finding out. Some starting points:

- Are you looking to nurture your idea, still fragile and in its infancy? You might be looking for generative feedback and validation, someone with an opinion that could expand your vision for the idea, and to give you energy to run with it. In this case, a supportive friend or a coach might be the best person to ask.
- Are you looking to refine your work? Peer feedback from someone else in a similar stage to your creative journey, familiar with your craft, who can make educated suggestions and ask the right questions might be

---

119. https://sive.rs/nod

your best bet. Ask them to focus on a specific part of your work, and
come prepared with specific questions for them.

- Are you preparing to submit your work somewhere, or to release it to
  the world? You might be looking for a candid and critical opinion from
  a potential stakeholder, tapping into someone else's inner judge and
  asking at least one question you're terrified to ask.

- Are you looking to promote your work? You might be looking less for
  feedback, and more commitment from an influential figure. It would
  be wise to make sure you've supported and promoted their work before
  you ask them for a favor. (Check out Groove founder Alex Turnbull's
  very comprehensive post[120] on the topic.)

- Want to know how a group responds to your work, what conversations
  they have with each other in response? You might be interested in
  throwing a feedback party, sharing your idea with as many people as
  possible and getting their quick impression of whether or not something resonates.

The next step is to actually identify the person. You may or may not
know them. If you don't, then it would make sense to at least reach out
first, probably to introduce yourself, before you ask them to give you some
of their time to provide feedback.

The third step is to ask. My personal preferred way of doing this is
simply to catch up and reconnect with a friend that I'm comfortable
with—who I've talked with about my writing before and who has shown
both emotional and promotional (and even financial!) support of my
work—and then to mention what I'm working on. I watch their body lan-
guage and listen to the questions they ask. If they seem curious about the
work, I'll probably ask, "Hey, can I run something by you?"

When you ask for feedback, you may think you're asking for a favor.
Okay, let's be honest, you definitely are asking for a favor. Still, that favor
may be exactly what the other person is looking for. As author and entrepreneur Derek Sivers writes in *Your Music, Your People,*[121] "You might
be the coolest thing that ever happened to a teenager going through an
unpopular phase. You might help someone start a new life after a break-

---

120. https://www.groovehq.com/blog/1000-subscribers

121. https://sive.rs/

up. You can provide some exciting variety to their boring routines." Thank you, and you're welcome.[122]

Maybe you're an artist who recently reconnected with a friend who studied art history and is working an unrelated full-time job. Or maybe you're a novelist who just found out your friend has made a new year's resolution to start reading more fiction this year.

While I've provided just a handful of starting points for asking for feedback, you can get super creative with how you receive it. For example, when Carly Rae Jepsen wrote 200 songs for her albums *Emotion* and *Dedicated*, she invited family and friends over for a listening party. She describes the process,[123] "We have these listening parties at my house where I feed everyone and give them copious amounts of wine hoping that they'll have opinions about the music. And then they all send in their votes to me, including my bandmates, my manager, and girlfriend Alex—she sends me notes in the night. There starts to be at least six to eight common songs that are all resonating with people. Then I pick the rest myself from my favorites and fill in the blanks of what's missing from the album."

11.6 *Release in a Lab*

Typically, creative work takes place in what psychologist Fabra Robin Hogarth calls a "wicked learning environment." These are environments that involve many variables, which make correlations and causations difficult to form. Predictions are very difficult to clearly make.

In this case, you want to release your work in a kind, closed, learning environment. This prompt calls for you to show your work to 10 different people. Ask 10 of them the same questions, and you'll start to see patterns. If you're uncertain of which questions to ask, try this ABCD framework from novelist Mary Robinette Kowal:[124]

- What's **A**wesome?
- What's **B**oring?
- What's **C**onfusing?

---

122. https://www.goodreads.com/book/show/6434804-thank-you-and-you-re-welcome

123. https://www.vox.com/2020/5/26/21266663/
     carly-rae-jepsen-dedicated-side-b-switched-on-pop

124. https://twitter.com/shl/status/1237132966414802944

- What **D**idn't you believe?

"What didn't you believe?" may be most helpful when responding to fiction, but disbelief is a form of distraction—a part of a story that I simply can't believe. So if "What didn't you believe?" doesn't seem like the right question for your work, you may ask, "What is distracting?" In other words, you're looking for elements of your work that take away from what you're trying to express.

Listen to or read their answers carefully. Or, if you can see them in person, watch their nonverbal reactions. Do their faces look impassive, or concentrated? Are their shoulders pointing away from the work or towards? Sit back and don't say anything. The silence is supposed to be there. There's no need to judge exactly what's happening, but do take note of the reactions.

The only variable that changes should be the person. Hold as many other variables constant as possible. Time of day. Place. The piece of work should be the same (don't make edits or revisions between feedback interviews). You may be surprised at what you learn, and how good a gauge even a small group of people can be. If you're interested in learning more about how to get feedback, check out how product designers do it.[125] There may be some methods that serve you.

11.7 *Share Your Intention*

On occasion, an intention[§13.1]—a reason, or a purpose, or even just a hypothesis—can be enough to get an idea started. When you share your intention, you give the other person or people a chance to make sense of it, which refines it and provides a space for it to grow.

It can help to be clearer with how you're asking someone to support your intention. I remember once introducing two friends over coffee, and one was sharing a vision of setting up a dome installation during a film festival and making a request for the other's expertise with cameras. I left in awe of my friend's informal presentation and vision.

Perhaps the request isn't supporting an end result, but for support during the process. For example, "I'm planning on writing for 100 days, and I'd love your support because I'm trying to be an author and it's going to be

---

125. https://trydesignlab.com/blog/how-to-ask-for-design-feedback-10-top-tips/

hard!" You might also make a request more specifically for accountability, or for feedback, or just general moral support.

Setting your intention and action in the right direction will help create momentum. Communicating that intention and showing people your work will get others involved. Given enough time and space, someone will see it and suggest a way they can contribute. Don't limit your vision to your work to yourself. Invite family and friends, friends of friends, and acquaintances to experience your work, and allow them a chance to understand and further your intention.

11.8 *Discard Some Feedback*

Early into his career as a designer at Adobe, Andrei Herasimchuk had designed and programmed[126] a prototype over the weekend and a few days into his workweek. One of the product managers, who had worked at Adobe for a while and was well liked by the team, stopped by Harsimchuk's cubicle.

After a question on how long this took, they said, "While I certainly applaud your effort, I must say that you really don't need to go to this length. You'll have to do this all the time for all the products going forward. These screenshots you have here are plenty. It's all we've ever done before, so there's really no need to spend this kind of time on a prototype."

Herasimchuk identifies the point when things went wrong, which is when he accepted the product manager's feedback blindly, "Um... Ok. I guess. If you think so." He never built another prototype while working at Adobe. His coding skills would dull over five years, and he missed a chance to make coding a part of Adobe's design culture.

Listening to other people's feedback is important—for certain. But as it turns out, they just might not understand your work. Or, they might not have been deliberate and thoughtful about your situation. If that's the case, it would be terrible for you to limit yourself because of one person's off-handed comment about your work or your process.

Throw out something that somebody else had said. Don't listen to it. If someone has told you they don't like seeing this part of your work, and you've cut it out, try to put it back in. If you're looking for a place to start,

---

126. https://medium.com/twenty-years-in-the-valley/
    one-of-the-biggest-mistakes-i-ve-made-in-my-career-72bf27c538b4

throw out the piece of feedback that drains your personal energy, and makes you feel less excited about your work.

PART III: CREATIVE PURPOSE

Creative expression involves physical, mental, and emotional contributions. I like to represent these as the hands, the head, and the heart. The prompts in this book so far have helped you align your hands and your head. Beginning with the hands means focusing on *practicing* creative work. With your hands, you focus on quantity over quality, creating many average successes and total failures, learning what works and what doesn't. By making many things, we let our expectations of each one melt away. We accept the truth that in order to make something great, we must start with the courage to make and release many ordinary things. The hands don't have an ego. The hands don't compare. The hands don't wonder what they don't know. They learn by doing, they test and experiment and try. And by putting our trust in our hands, whatever unworthiness or intimidation we feel in our heads and hearts is quieted, and our creative confidence grows.

As we progress in cultivating a hands-focused creative process, we've also developed expectations and a growing sense of what "quality" means to us and our work. Maybe we've defined what we want to create by trying many things, studying the creators, works, and stories that came before us, and speculating on what may come after us. Our studios bear a close resemblance to scientific laboratories. We've begun to deliberately choose our style and direction, and decide how to practice our creative operations.

The prompts in this final section will work to align your heart with your head and hands. Our hearts provide us with the spirit and energy we need to keep our hands and heads adapting. When we work with our hearts, our creative process takes us deep into ourselves, and we start to make sense of the parts of our lives we forgot or didn't notice before. We start seeing why things happened, what drives our obsessions, and what makes us who we really are. It's in finding, connecting with, and expressing these deep, universal, truths that we create opportunities to build deep connections between ourselves and someone else. External expectations like reception, competition, and logistics fade away. Only completing the current phase of the exploration matters. In opening our hearts, our heads and hands will follow, and we tap into the deepest level of creative doing.

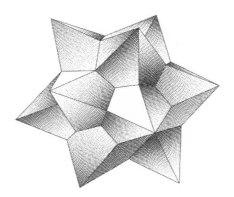

12 Get Out Of Your Own Way

Throughout the book, we've already alluded to breaking imaginary barriers,[§6.2] relaxing expectations,[§6.7] and losing ourselves.[§6.5] At this point in the journey, we will embrace letting go; to be gentle with ourselves and to seek a harmony with the creative process. In *What is Tao?*, Alan Watts describes a skilled carpenter saying, "Let the saw do the work, let the teeth do the cutting."

We'll learn to break the habit of force and discipline, and to accept and embrace how the work turns out, even if the outcome doesn't fit in with what we were expecting or preferring.

12.1 *Stop Obsessing*

As powerful as it is, obsession can also be a troubling occupation of the mind. Left unchecked, it also causes obstacles, or even causes projects—and people—to eventually self-destruct. Obsession can raise a standard so far beyond acceptable that nobody can meet it, creating a creative block. Many people become slaves to their obsessions, caving in to the impulse to push for perfection. Sometimes, if they're lucky, this results in a complete piece of work. Many other times, though, it causes the work to self-destruct.

The Pixar team, inarguably masters at the crafts of storytelling and animation, also face the over-obsession challenge. Sometimes, people on their team spend days or weeks on a detail that none of the viewers ever actually see. In the 2001 blockbuster *Monsters Inc.*, there is a three-second segment where Boo knocks over a stack of CDs.[127] Pixar artists created a CD cover, as well as a program to change rendering for each of over 90 CDs, for a three-second segment. It was a level of detail that very few, if any, viewers would notice. "Clearly, something in our process had broken—the desire for quality had gone well beyond rationality," writes Pixar co-founder Ed Catmull in *Creativity Inc.*[128]

We can practice loosening the grip obsession can have on us in the creative process. In practice, this means declaring something that you feel is acceptable[§9.3]—but incomplete—to be done. If it's not acceptable, scope it down by omitting the incomplete details.

If you really can't bring yourself to do this—if only it were so easy!—set a timer for 45 minutes to complete the omissions and transition the rest of the work together, and declare the work done after the timer goes off. Save and title this version of the work.

If you're still not happy with it, pick up where you'd started and create a different version tomorrow. Treat the detail or aspect that you're obsessing over like a brand new starting point for different versions of your work each day.

127. https://www.youtube.com/watch?v=-2fmN4E0DK0

128. https://books.google.com/books?id=UqccAgAAQBAJ&pg=PT197

Make notes of the process, including how letting go feels, what you're afraid of, what imperfection means to you, and what you're comfortable and not comfortable compromising on. Through this journaling process, you'll learn the aspects of obsession that are driving you and getting in the way of you relaxing, and doing your best work as a result.

↦ **Or flip this prompt:** *Obsess over Details*§9.9

12.2 *Know Your Stage*

In 1926, London School of Economics co-founder Graham Wallas published The Art of Thought, in which he described a four-stage creative process. The first three stages were adapted from physicist Hermann von Helmholtz, and Wallas's descriptions are in quotes:

Preparation: "the stage during which the problem was 'investigated ... in all directions'"—think about exercises, rituals, and routines that stimulate your mind.

Incubation: "not consciously thinking about the problem"—this is about consciously letting go of the problem and relaxing your mind. It might involve going for a walk in nature, or relaxing in a shower.

Illumination: "the appearance of the 'happy idea' together with the psychological events which immediately preceded and accompanied that appearance"—the eureka moment, where an answer comes to you, either quietly or striking like a bolt of lightning.

Verification: "the validity of the idea was tested, and the idea itself was reduced to exact form"—the phase where an illumination is tested through feedback or, in science, proofs and matching theories.

Whether it's a 60-second speed writing exercise, or a song that takes 5,000 hours to perfect and record, every work goes through this linear process. You can look at any creative product through this lens. For example, virologist Jonas Salk spent his preparation phase cooped up in his windowless basement laboratory at Pittsburgh Municipal Hospital, working 16-hour days to figure out the polio vaccine.[129] In exhaustion, Salk entered his incubation phase, retreating to the monastery at the Basilica

---

129. https://www.cbsnews.com/news/the-salk-polio-vaccine-a-medical-miracle-turns-60/

of San Francesco d'Assisi in Italy, a magnificent structure permeated by natural light. That's where the illumination happened. Of course, Salk attributed the discovery to his environment—but it's important to consider that he was taking a break when the breakthrough happened. And lastly, the verification phase: in addition to testing two children at two Pittsburgh-area institutions, Salk injected himself and his family with the vaccine in his kitchen.

While most processes have start and end phases, in the creative process, a verification stage may also double as a preparation stage of a different project, which then starts a new cycle. Some people, upon getting new ideas for their project near the finish line, grow reluctant to draw their work to a close. That's how the creative process can go on forever; it's our job to draw it to a temporary close.

The value of the work is recognized when a version of the work is deemed finished. We must make the infinite finite. It is possible to update and iterate—many books have revised editions (like this one!), many albums get remastered and remixed—but the original work needs to be complete enough for people to watch, touch, listen to, taste, read, see, or experience in some other way. For example, you might find that getting the resources and support you need to make the best version of a book happens only after you complete and publish an article on the topic. That's when the creative process can be seen as linear, for a single piece of work. A separate creative process can start over again once you decide to turn that article into a book.

Seeing this linear process is the key to understanding how to make each piece of creative work happen. The process can be straightforward and simple, like an assembly line. From this perspective, the goal of your creative process is to create a steady, predictable, and uninterrupted flow of creative work. Your creative process also should prevent you from getting blocked, fixated, or tormented by the excitement of new ideas or fixation on perfection.

12.3 *Identify Your Bottleneck*

In his 1984 business fable *The Goal*, Eliyahu M. Goldratt wrote about how any improvements or optimizations made to a single process are an illusion, unless they're at the bottleneck. This is often the *slowest* step, or the *weakest* link. In their book *Diaminds: Decoding the Mental Habits of Successful Thinkers*, Mihnea Moldoveanu and Roger Martin describe this constraint as a "rate-limiting step," and illustrate it with the example of the flexion hip joint, which gets in the way of even the fastest sprinter from being even faster.

This idea applies to your own creative process. It's important to take a critical eye to your work and assess which part of the process is limiting you. If you're not happy with your results, it's easy to blame an absence of audiences or an unfavorable algorithm. But both of those are lagging indicators of high potential creative work and the promotional work that activates the potential.

Here's a list of questions you can ask yourself to see which stage you're getting stuck in the creative process, at the preparation, incubation, illumination, or verification stages:

1. *If it's a struggle for you to come up with enough ideas, expand your preparation phase. Find more references and spend time studying them and distinguishing between the ones you like and don't like, and why. (See Visit the Greats.$^{\S9.4}$)*

2. *If you find you're coming up with a lot of ideas, but none are resonating, expand your incubation phase. Give your brain more time to rest and relax. (See Make Idle Time.$^{\S6.3}$)*

3. *If you find you're missing breakthroughs, pay more attention. Write each breakthrough down whenever you feel your mind making a connection, whether it's a small one or a big one. Don't distinguish or edit what your mind is telling you. (See Write Down 10 Ideas.$^{\S8.1}$)*

4. *If you find that you don't have enough time and energy to make acceptable work,$^{\S9.3}$ redefine what quality means^{§9} to you at this point in your life. In all likelihood, you have to assess how much time, money, energy, and other resources you have to verify—edit, polish, refine, design—and lower the fidelity and scope you are shipping your ideas with. (See Complete Your Operation in Seconds.$^{\S7.7}$)*

This last one is what I wrestle with the most. I tend to write pretty quickly, but I find it time consuming to come up with new, relevant ideas$^{\S8.1}$ and pitch them to publications. This is the step I need to work on.

In order to continue supporting myself and strengthening my pitches, I'll need to cultivate different sources, ones that spread news or share interesting perspectives faster. I need to focus my efforts into specific areas and use relevant events to speak to that area. I'm considering coming up with a weekly or even daily quota of article ideas that I pitch every day.

Since your situation is specific to you, I'll suggest a few questions as starting points to get you to take a step back and look at your creative process:

1. *Dive deeper into these phases, especially if you find yourself getting stuck in one specific part. For example, you may find that your brain is out of practice with getting its unfiltered, unedited, incomplete, thoughts out there. You can then start designing your own exercises for this. (See Julia Cameron's morning pages in Commit to a Size,$^{\S7.3}$ and the journaling exercise in Stop Obsessing$^{\S12.1}$) Nobody else will read this. What's on your mind? What are you feeling? What is clear and unclear to you?*

2. *Think about thinking. Write down and listen to what your mind and body are telling you about a specific constraint. For example, is it expressing a fear of embarrassment? Or a skepticism that what you're about to do is not worth doing? What emotion are you experiencing? What activities are you occupying yourself with instead of your creative work?*

3. *Advise someone else in the same situation. If your friend or peer was approaching you with this problem, what observation would you make about where they were getting stuck? What would you say to them?*

4. *Talk to a friend, or to yourself, about this question: Which part is the most painful part of the creative process for you? Why?*

Through answering these questions, you can look into the section that you've identified, and pay attention the next time you go through the process. What is holding you up? What feels bad? What is your action, or reaction, that blocks you?

12.4 *Be Obvious*

This prompt actually emerged as my own reflection, as I was identifying my bottleneck.[§12.3] For example, I'm fairly practiced at writing ideas down, but I have a difficult time choosing one to start writing. I realized through listening to myself that one of the blocks I face as an author is, "I don't want to write this, it's too obvious." This feeling of a lack of originality is a challenge that I've seen other writers face as well.

For me, I came across a few sources of consolation. First off, I saw a tweet[130] from marketer and software engineer Patrick McKenzie assuring the reader, "You radically underestimate both a) how much you know that other people do not and b) the instrumental benefits to you of publishing it." McKenzie also linked to New Science executive director and blogger Alexey Guzey's writing about the value of unoriginality,[131] "Because it helps in the process of discovery and in the process of supporting underappreciated ideas."

I also noticed how a handful of "obvious" ideas other people had made an impact on me and my friends. For me, two examples were author Seth Godin's "Talker's Block"[132]—which asks why writer's block exists when nobody gets talker's block—and Roy Bahat's "Forwardable email,"[133] which suggests that readers shouldn't ask for an email introduction, and instead make a request for someone to forward their email along.

I grew to appreciate that what was obvious to me might not be so obvious to someone else, and might seem original and—more importantly—useful.

Don't worry about factors that aren't limiting you. Work on the step that slows you down the most, whichever it is. Once you've identified the step, you can isolate it, then study it for a few weeks. If you're looking externally, you can find someone who has dealt with a similar challenge before, and through their public appearances or documentation on social media (or reaching out for an informational interview), find out what they do to solve it—whether it's physical or a mental workaround—and select some insights to take back with you and apply into your own constraint.

---

130. https://twitter.com/patio11/status/936638517676974080
131. https://guzey.com/personal/why-have-a-blog/#
    a-note-on-your-ideas-feeling-less-original-than-they-actually-are
132. https://seths.blog/2011/09/talkers-block/
133. https://also.roybahat.com/introductions-and-the-forward-intro-email-14e2827716a1

Put those insights into practice into your own creative process, as new routines or rituals.

12.5 *Embarrass Yourself*

We choose creative work not only because we love it; we also have good taste. Naturally, as we start making creative work, we see the distance between what we call good and what we're making. The fear dawns on us: What if *we* make something bad?

This is the gap between taste and ability that everyone starts with. As broadcaster and producer Ira Glass says,[134] "It's only by actually going through a volume of work that you're actually going to catch up and close that gap. The work you're making will be as good as your ambitions."

The *quantity* of work is essential. We'll make mistakes, pretend we know what we're doing, say the wrong things, imitate people, and find new ways of working that we swore we'd never do.

We need to set the expectation with ourselves that we will probably look foolish as we make our early work. In fact, we need to lean into it and accept it.

There's also another reason we'll look foolish, even as we start to emerge as artists and creators. "To the preservation of the universe, instead of its destruction," poet Allen Ginsberg said. He and conservative political commentator William F. Buckley, Jr., were debating the Vietnam War. Ginsberg pulled a harmonium up, sat it on his lap, and sang a Hare Krishna song.[135] Buckley Jr. smiled the smile of someone uncertain of how to react. As Allen sang seriously, Buckley Jr.'s smile disappeared, and he moved a finger over his mouth as if to silence himself. Unwilling to offer his approval, Buckley Jr. laughed after the song, "That was the most un-*Hare Kirshna* I've ever heard."

---

134. https://www.youtube.com/watch?v=X2wLP0izeJE

135. https://www.youtube.com/watch?v=vBpoZBhvBa4

In a TED Talk,[136] actor and director Ethan Hawke described Ginsberg returning to New York City after this performance to his friends—his fellow Beats—rebuking him for the song. He looked like an idiot, they said, and the whole country was making fun of him.

Ginsberg responded, "That's my job, and I'm going to play the fool."

The ensuing embarrassment, shame, or even humiliation, that comes from being made to feel stupid can feel overwhelming and intolerable. Our minds evolve to protect us from this emotional pain, as well as the ensuing real-world consequences. Yet in the early stages of creative work, you must be willing to look foolish and vulnerable. You must be willing to look silly, and to try. You'll also learn not to identify yourself with an idea or moment in which you appeared foolish to someone else.

So, do something embarrassing. Express something honest, something positive, that you think may be silly.

As filmmaker David Lynch wrote, "Keep your eye on the doughnut, not on the hole." Stay focused on the work and what you want to say. Don't be afraid of how people may or may not react—be okay with making them laugh at you, not with you. Know that in the quiet hour when they can't sleep, your truth may come into their mind, and they'll wonder what it all really meant.

12.6 *Make a Risky Version of Your Work*

One of the best things you can do with and for your creative practice is to get outside your comfort zone and exercise your capacity for creative risk. Think of it like the director's cut of a film. As Marina Abramović wrote in *Walk Through Walls*, "I always question artists who are successful in whatever they do. I think what that means is that they're repeating themselves and not taking enough risks."

"Safe" means creating something you're most familiar with, that is, your "style." Making something risky might mean dialing your style up to the maximum, or flipping it to be the complete opposite. Or it might just mean doing something completely out of the blue—that exceeds my capacity for suggestion.

For example, my friends told me that writing without quotes makes for better writing. This had paralyzed me for a bit—until I decided that

---

136. https://www.youtube.com/watch?v=WRS9Gek4V5Q

I'd eventually just create two versions of this draft of the book, one with no quotes and one with all quotes. Similarly, I'd been stuck on structure, until I realized that I could just create a different version of the book with a completely different structure, perhaps a more essay-related format. I had no idea when I released this how it was going to look—and that was okay. That was how it was supposed to be.

Creative rituals, routines, and themes make it easy to get into a creative groove. But ease isn't the goal, excellence is.

A certain degree of risk is a necessary ingredient in tapping into, and feeding, the chaotic energy of creativity.[§8.3] The risk could result in something original, which pushes the previously self-imposed boundaries of your work and pushes you to perceive or express yourself in a new way.

↠ **Or flip this prompt:** *Find Your Comfort*[§12.10]

12.7 *Archive an Idea*

Choose an idea to put away. Don't look at it again for at least six months. This prompt is particularly useful if you're struggling with developing an idea; get out of your own way and let time do the work for you by archiving it.

The late Intel chief Andy Grove writes of a simple rule in *High Output Management*: "All production flows have a basic characteristic: the material becomes more valuable as it moves through the process." That's because more time and energy have been spent on the material to make it a final product.

One implication of this idea is the earlier you stop working on something, the fewer resources you waste. For example, if I'm coming up with a pitch, a quick Google search could tell me if someone else has written about the thing I want to write about. If someone has, in exactly the way I wanted to write about it, then I can easily shelve the idea in its current state, as it's not acceptable[§9.3] to me. If I didn't come across the prior coverage until later in my process, I'd have to give up the idea after hours spent researching and writing (which has happened before).

Sometimes, a challenging idea may be worth producing. But it takes clear discernment and deliberation to decide if that's the case. A safer strategy could be to simply shelve the idea, and revisit it again in six months—perhaps time will be your ally and your subconscious mind will conceive of a new way to reframe your idea.

There is no right way to choose an idea to put away, or to pick back up. Just choose!

↦ **Or flip this prompt:** *Pick a Neglected Idea*[§8.8]

12.8 *Praise Your Own Work*

What would you think about your work if you didn't know your own intentions or disappointments?

Too often, our uncertainty of our work leads us to be critical of ourselves. We say things to or about ourselves that we never would accept other people saying to us, nor that we would say about others. "I believe that unless combated, self-hate is easy to develop and nearly impossible to shed," writes Donda West in her book *Raising Kanye*.

However, we also have the ability to choose and take action. We can flip that tendency on its head. Be your own greatest supporter.

This prompt isn't just about making ourselves feel good, it's about nurturing and developing your own talent, recognizing progress, understanding what's working in what you do, and identifying where you excel. When you do this, you can then focus on improving other aspects of your craft, or drawing out what's truly special about your talent.

Look at a completed version of your work and write down five things that are working well. Here are some potential starting points:

- If you have been practicing or developing a certain technique, analyze your development and how it contributes to the piece. (For example, if you'd been practicing crosshatching—did it improve in this piece? For me, maybe I've been practicing writing headlines—does this headline pique my own curiosity, more so than the ones I'd written previously?)
- Reflect on your process. If you set out to work consistently, did you meet your goal? If you're setting out to explore new or groundbreaking subject matter, are you getting closer to that?
- What did you learn from this week's work sessions? Are there lessons you've learned outside your creative process that you can apply to it?
- What would a supportive friend say about this? What would an imaginary biggest fan say? What would a family member say?

- How do the lessons you've learned and your current work set you up for the future? What are some directions it can take you in, towards where you want to go?

This encouragement is a foundation for continued action. You can throw grandiose admiration onto your work, loudly praising yourself for it. Or perhaps quietly appreciate it. After all, it takes support to nurture and continue on a mission and to keep the main thing the main thing.

12.9 *Accept Imperfection*

One powerful antidote to over-obsession[§12.1] is accepting that imperfection is the essence of nature itself. The Japanese philosophy of *wabi sabi* embodies this theme. Author Beth Kempton translates the two words in her book, *Wabi Sabi: Japanese Wisdom for a Perfectly Imperfect Life*: "*Wabi* is about finding beauty in simplicity, and a spiritual richness and serenity in detaching from the material world. *Sabi* is more concerned with the passage of time, with the way that all things grow and decay and how aging alters the visual nature of those things."

With the understanding of the etymology, Kempton describes the concept the two words convey:

> *Wabi sabi is an intuitive response to beauty that reflects the true nature of life.*
> *Wabi sabi is an acceptance and appreciation of the impermanent, imperfect, and incomplete nature of everything.*
> *Wabi sabi is a recognition of the gifts of simple, slow, and natural living.*
> *Wabi sabi is a state of the heart. It is a deep in-breath and a slow exhale. It is felt in a moment of real appreciation—a perfect moment in an imperfect world.*

We must accept that each imperfection is not a failure; rather, in *wabi sabi* fashion, each one makes the piece perfectly imperfect. Otherwise, obsession becomes a prescription for failure. An expectation or obsession for quality does not necessarily always result in it.

12.10 *Find Your Comfort*

To take risks and get out of your comfort zone has practically become a virtue of modern life. This book is no exception to that, with prompts on releasing your work, getting feedback, and exploring your own creative capacity.

As your journey continues, you might find that finding a ritual, prompt, or environment that makes you comfortable can support you in exploring your art and maintaining your creative process. Finding your comfort means noticing when you get into the groove with the work, and potentially developing warm-up routines to support that.

Michelle Kuo says being relaxed during the creative process is really important. "It's not pure relaxation, it's like relaxation plus a little bit of tension," she says in an interview for this book. "I was taking these singing classes. I really adored my singing teacher, and she used to say this thing that always stuck with me, which is: to hit the high notes you have to be relaxed. Most people tense up when they see a high note coming, but actually to hit it, your breath needs to be relaxed."

Finding your comfort could also mean acknowledging your own progress. "The more I've been painting, I don't know if I'll be getting better, but I get a lot more comfortable. When you're a lot more comfortable, I think you are getting a lot better," says Michael Saviello. "Your technique is improving even though you don't know it."

↔ **Or flip this prompt:** *Make a Risky Version of Your Work*§12.6

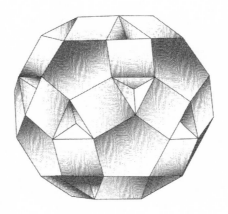

13 Know Your Why

"If you don't stand for something, you'll fall for anything."

— Unknown

Have you ever wondered why the comic strip *Calvin and Hobbes* only exists on the printed page? Unlike Snoopy or Mickey Mouse, there are no blockbuster movies, no Netflix specials, and certainly no stuffed animals. Nobody even knows what Calvin's or Hobbes's voices sound like. That's the result of a deliberate decision that the cartoon's creator Bill Watterson made to not license out his work.

Watterson's former business partners (the staff at a syndicate responsible for putting *Calvin and Hobbes* in the newspapers), estimate that tens, if not hundreds, of millions of dollars could have been made should Watterson have licensed *Calvin and Hobbes*. But for years, Watterson fought not to, and eventually won out.

At least partially, the decision was practical; Watterson said,[137] "No one cartoonist has the time to write and draw a daily strip and do all the work

---

137. http://www.brunothebandit.com/watterson.html

of a licensing program." But the refusal to license his work was a philosophical stance as well. In *Exploring Calvin and Hobbes*, Watterson wrote, "The artist gets to decide what his own creation is about and stands for. If licensing fits your vision of your creation, wonderful, go nuts. But I reserve the option of saying no for my own work. If I don't like licensing, I should be allowed to refuse it. That's all it was."

We may not have hundreds of millions of dollars at stake, but we do have dilemmas and decisions to make every day related to our own ideas of our integrity. Should we try to get the promotion, or should we put more time into our creative work? Should we incorporate feedback to try to make our work more popular, or should we stay true to our original vision?

In his commencement speech to Kenyon College, Watterson talked about these decisions, and advocated defining what success and happiness mean for you. He urged listeners not to confuse being happy with being enviable, and said,[138] "Creating a life that reflects your values and satisfies your soul is a rare achievement."

13.1 *Set an Intention*

Each of us has an impulse to make excellent things, to tinker, and to seek fulfillment and reward. We may also feel a need to express ourselves in order to gain a sense of comprehension or fulfillment. We want to tell our stories, like we have for hundreds of years, to make something that has a chance of lasting beyond our finite human lives, as well as to make a bid to connect with other people. We may also be driven by a deeper mission or through-line, to support or honor something or someone. We may want to give back to our community, or to find more fulfillment and reward in our jobs.

As you move forward, gaining momentum, you'll face countless obstacles. You will need to do a simple, but very difficult, thing, which is to set an intention for your work. This transcends practice, technique, and experiments. What are you doing, and why are you doing it?

If we don't make time to reflect on why we are creating, then political, economic, and social incentives all have a way of seeping in and causing

---

138. https://web.mit.edu/jmorzins/www/C-H-speech.html

us to make decisions based on their values. As Watterson said,[139] "Selling out is usually more a matter of buying in. Sell out, and you're really buying into someone else's system of values, rules and rewards."

The solution I propose here is an intention—your own position on what you want to do. In order to do that, you need to have an idea of your purpose as well. I know there are plenty of books out there that talk about how to do this, but my opinion is they complicate the whole matter. Nobody, no framework, no prompt, can figure out why except for you, so the only thing left to do is for you to do it and trust that you'll figure it out along the way. Or as Ethan Hawke says,[140] "There is no path till you walk it."

13.2 *Set a Mission*

Commercial success and acceptance are both outside of your control. Aiming at those goals would be like trying to aim at the wind, instead of trying to ride with it and have it fill your sails.

Rather than succeed commercially, set out to do something for yourself. It could be as simple as trying to have as much fun as possible. As renowned record producer and recording artist Pharrell Williams says,[141] "As long as I concentrate on the fun, it usually turns out cool. It's when I become too worried about how it has to be, that's when God spends a lot of time chuckling at me."

Maybe you are setting out to express or expose some sort of truth, or to discover it, and to figure it out. Or you're just trying to refine your techniques. Whatever it is—make it an internal mission, and not an external one.

Another way to say this is to develop a through-line for your current project. The through-line is at the heart of your project. In his class for Skillshare,[142] author and restaurateur Eddie Huang likens a through-line to a thesis, and describes the through-line for his restaurant Baohaus dri-

---

139. https://web.mit.edu/jmorzins/www/C-H-speech.html

140. https://www.youtube.com/watch?v=WRS9Gek4V5Q

141. https://www.npr.org/about-npr/452953953/
     transcript-pharrell-williams-in-conversation-with-nyu-tisch-npr-music

142. https://s3.amazonaws.com/skillshare/assets/hybrid/project-briefs/Project+Brief_Eddie_
     Final.pdf

ven by the truth, "No one would kick you out, call the cops, or serve you shitty 7-Eleven pressed Cubans."

On a trip to Japan, Momofuku founder David Chang stumbled upon an insight. He writes in *Eat a Peach*, "I could eat extraordinarily well in places that weren't punishingly expensive." Later on, he adds, "The way people ate in train stations, shopping malls, back alleys, and strip malls in Asia was superior to the way we ate in upscale New York restaurants." This insight would be the through-line for Momofuku: "That was the big idea: leave everyone walking out the door of Momofuku happy and surprised and glad to have spent their money." The rest of the themes we identify with Momofuku—innovative food, the decor, the service, and everything else—were driven by this simple through-line, the heartbeat of Momofuku's restaurants.

If you're struggling through this, don't just write one mission (or through-line) down. Write everything down that comes to mind, without thinking too much about it. At this stage, it should really just be a single sentence. Write down 100 sentences, 100 missions. If it takes more than a couple of hours, you're thinking too much. Allow the mission to emerge from the quantity—let yourself be drawn.

After writing 100 missions, if you still don't have anything, re-read them, and pick the ten that resonate most with you. Make the case for each of them, by answering some of these questions:

- Why is this mission important to you?
- What idea or experience inspired you to take on this mission?
- What will the world look like after you accomplish your mission?
- Can you imagine the world without you accomplishing your proposed mission?
- Who or what does your mission serve? Who or what will your mission honor?

These questions are merely starting points for you to explore your ten most resonant missions. From there, pick one. (If you're feeling really stuck, you can enlist the help of a friend and make the case *against* each one—to start eliminating missions. Or, if you're feeling spontaneous, roll the dice.[§8.3])

Eventually, you may be able to even boil it down to a single word and hang it above your worktable.

↩ **Or flip this prompt:** *Sell Out*[§10.5]

13.3 *Ignore the Stats*

Everyone creates for different reasons; some of us might do it to be seen, read, heard, or felt. And while this deep connection can be incredibly rewarding and meaningful, the pressure of increasing expectations, social engagement, and sales that often represent it can crush the joy out of creativity.

Before author Mason Currey published his *Daily Rituals* series of books, he says in an interview with me, "I had, literally, 12 readers for like a year and a half. It was just my coworkers and my family." His first book, *Daily Rituals: How Artists Work*, has now been reviewed over 17,000 times on Goodreads.[143] When I asked artist Shantell Martin—who has 250,000 followers across YouTube and Instagram—about her analytics, she said, "I don't pay any attention to that stuff."

"The most important thing I can tell you is to relish writing in obscurity," author Michelle Kuo said to me in an interview. "I feel that I was the happiest as a writer when I was in hiding, when I was invisible, when I was secretly writing, stealing away portions of time at work, or writing on scraps of paper, or forming sentences in my head on the commute. That was a time before I had published really anything and before I even thought my writing would become a book, I was just trying to organize or to create order in my emotional life."

Kuo recalls focusing, instead, on simpler metrics: "Am I writing?" "Am I showing up?" "Am I discovering something new about these experiences or about this world?" "Am I having new encounters alone?" These types of qualitative metrics, more grounded in the process than the outcome, will enable you to get back to what really matters: your creative work. Remember to enjoy the plateau.[§6.6]

---

143. https://www.goodreads.com/book/show/15799151-daily-rituals

13.4 *See the Vision*

Martial artist George Leonard quotes Arnold Schwarzenegger in his *Mastery*: "All I know is that the first step is to create the vision, because when you see the vision there—the beautiful vision—that creates the 'want power.' For example, my wanting to be Mr. Universe came about because I saw myself so clearly, being up there on the stage and winning."

Picture the final version of your project, or the specific accomplishment you want. You can put it all on a vision board, collaging images of your vision together. Or, you can write it down in your journal. You can also make it more formal and concrete, writing it down as a press release like the Amazon team does.[144]

Align your energy all towards the same goal. Aim it. And then fire. Or, in Zen fashion, forget about the goal, and let the unconscious deal with it.§7.4

13.5 *Keep Moving Forward*

> "*Most people overestimate what they can do in one year and underestimate what they can do in ten years.*"
>
> — A popular saying[145]

Donald Glover was a screenwriter for *30 Rock* and played the beloved character Troy on *Community*, and his work has since earned him several Grammys, Golden Globes, and Emmy awards. Glover is a polymath. When he released his first official album as Childish Gambino, *Camp*, a critic at Pitchfork gave it a scathing review[146] and a score of 1.6/10.

It's not difficult to imagine how I might feel in such a situation—disappointed, embarrassed, and discouraged—at such a public rejection of what I had worked so hard on. And yet, whether it was due to his commitments or his drive, Glover kept moving forward with his music career even though he experienced so much success as a writer and comedian. It would have been easy to quit and stick to his comfort zone, but he didn't.

---

144. https://www.quora.com/
    What-is-Amazons-approach-to-product-development-and-product-management/answer/
    Ian-McAllister
145. https://quoteinvestigator.com/2019/01/03/estimate/
146. https://pitchfork.com/reviews/albums/16074-camp/

He said,[147] "I don't even really understand what I'm doing. I don't. And I don't think anybody great understands what they're doing, hopefully. I don't think they do."

Dacoury Natche, who has worked with Donald Glover on his album *3.15.20*, spoke to me in an interview for this book about his beliefs that great prolific work is fueled by inspiration and a connection to culture. Mixtape runs in hip-hop are a great example of this, whether it's Lil' Wayne's *Dedication* series, 50 Cent's pre-debut mixtapes, or Gucci Mane's many mixtapes. Natche's point reminds me of musicologist Neal Zaslaw, who writes[148] of Mozart's work, "Mozart did not compose because he was inspired, although inspiration may be why he composed so well."

Mixtapes are also a good example of inspiration paired up with the key element of consistency. Maria Popova, curator and creator of *Brain Pickings* (now *The Marginalian*), describes this as[149] "consistency driven by a deep love of the work." Consistency works best when you love the process. When you want to keep coming back to the work, you'll find consistency. You can only grit your teeth and march through hell for so long.

Consistency needs to be manageable. Complexity needs simplifying. Rigidness needs flexibility. And sometimes this means returning back to focus on doing the actions of your work every day.

"There is nothing stronger than those two: *patience and time*, they will do it all," Leo Tolstoy wrote in *War and Peace*.[150] When you allow time to do its work, instead of working against it and trying to aim for quick success, you can truly harness its power.

147. https://soundcloud.com/slava-p/donald-glover#t=1:28:30

148. https://www.researchgate.net/publication/274195289_Mozart_as_a_Working_Stiff

149. https://tim.blog/wp-content/uploads/2018/07/92-maria-popova.pdf

150. https://www.gutenberg.org/files/2600/2600-h/2600-h.htm

AFTERWORD

"Independent inquiry is needed in your search for truth, not dependence on anyone else's view or a mere book."

— Bruce Lee[151]

For me, the most valuable thing about creative doing is reiterating the role of action in thinking. We learn not only by thinking, we learn by doing. We set ourselves from the paralysis of analysis by taking action, which is something we knew as children and learn to stop doing as we grow up. If we want to be more creative, we need to reconnect with our inner instinct to make and be open to introducing some chaos into our structured lives.

Perhaps the ancient Roman civilization understood this. Their god Janus, whose domain involves time, beginnings and endings, and transitions, has a head with two faces. The creative process is, similarly, two sided. It involves structure and chaos, freedom and constraint, and spontaneity and consistency. Of course, it also involves both creative thinking and creative doing. To neglect one is to neglect the other. At the end of this book, I hope you get to restart your creative journey, if you haven't already. Spending more time on creative doing means improving the clarity and quality of your creative thinking.

It's in creative doing that we rediscover the joy of making for its own sake, find new sources of inspiration, and work through creative blocks. We also learn and apply the practical skills of carving time and space out of each day to make, creating safe spaces for people to brainstorm and come up with ideas, and find ways to solve problems old and new.

No matter how small or large, how simple or complex, always make something.

Please email me if you have any questions. herbert.be.lui@gmail.com

If you liked what you read, check out my newsletter, where I share the best of what I'm reading every month.[152]

---

151. Lee, Bruce. *Bruce Lee Striking Thoughts: Bruce Lee's Wisdom for Daily Living.* Tuttle Publishing, 2016, p. 209.

152. https://herbertlui.net/best-of-books

14 Acknowledgments

"Everything around you that you call life was made up by people that were no smarter than you."

— Steve Jobs[153]

Each opportunity to create provides us with a chance to become a part of something much larger than ourselves. Sometimes, creativity can even feel like a force channeling into us from the heavens, history, space, the infinite beyond. As recording artist Pharrell Williams said,[155] "We don't make much happen when it comes to creativity. We're just antennas and transistors. We're speakers. We're just lucky to get the transmission."

I wrote *Creative Doing* at home, mostly locked down during the COVID-19 pandemic. I'm still grateful that I had a chance to make it happen, and I couldn't have done it alone. Writing this book indeed allowed me to become part of something larger than myself. There are a lot of people who contributed to my creative doing:

First and foremost thank you Bernice for your support, inspiration, and for being a great partner. Thank you also for creating a beautiful cover of this book, discovering the original concept, and other much appreciated and unattributed guidance.

I'm grateful to work with the Holloway team to bring out the best version of this book. Rachel, thank you for being a strong organizing force and advocate for the concepts in this book, and for believing in the ideas and making so many contributions to it. Josh, thank you for believing in this book, for providing the Holloway platform and experience to get it out to more readers. Ben, thank you for your guidance with marketing. To Hope, Nat, and the Holloway team, thanks for your great work with the product.

And of course, *Creative Doing* is the second edition of my first book, *There Is No Right Way to Do This*, which my friends helped me ship. Tommy, thank you for your comments on the early sections of this book, and for instilling the craft of writing into your work, and mine. Michael, thank you for your feedback, ideas, and support. Ellen, thank you for

---

153. Interview with Steve Jobs, 1994.[154] Private interview by the Santa Clara Valley Historical Association.

154. https://www.youtube.com/watch?v=kYfNvmFoBqw

155. https://www.youtube.com/watch?v=PnahkJevp64

proofreading and catching the very big mistakes, as well as the details I would have missed. Faiz and Joey, thank you for your friendship and for reading early copies of this. Rob, Farhan, Vishaal, Moe, thank you for your feedback, friendship, and answers as I was first researching the idea of the book.

To the creative doers I interviewed—Dacoury Natche, Michelle Kuo, Shantell Martin, Vin Verma, Lindsay Jean Thomson, Alex Kallaway, Vincent Pan, Chris Kim, Rob Wang, Mason Currey, and Michael Saviello—thank you for taking the time to speak with me and share your expertise for the book. It wouldn't be the same without you. You are inspiring.

Ms Eckersley and Mr. Johnston, thank you both for being the life-changing teachers that you are. To my friends, thank you for supporting me from near and far.

Ray, thank you for your support, experience, and counsel.

Mom and dad, thank you for your love, support, and good habits. This book probably wouldn't exist without the visits to bookstores, libraries, and book fairs.

15 More About the Artists

Mason Currey is the author of the *Daily Rituals* books, featuring brief profiles of the day-to-day working lives of more than 300 great creative minds. If he didn't start the genre, Mason definitely popularized public interest in routines, which I've found to really benefit my creative process.

Alex Kallaway is the lead developer at Jiffy. He started the #100DaysOf-Code challenge, a must-try for anyone wanting to refine their programming skills.

Chris Kim (CVRE) is a multi-instrumentalist, producer, songwriter and sound designer whose work has been used in tracks by artists like Justin Bieber, A Boogie With Da Hoodie, Future, Juice WRLD, and Don Toliver. Rob, Vinny, and Chris started Good Karma.[156]

---

156. https://wewantgoodkarma.com/

Michelle Kuo is an Associate Professor in the History, Law, and Society program at the American University of Paris, and a visiting professor at National Taiwan University. She is the author of *Reading with Patrick*, based on her experiences teaching English in the heart of the Mississippi Delta at an alternative school for kids who were expelled from other schools and returning to work as a tutor in a county jail after graduating from Harvard Law School. Michelle's writing has changed my life and it will change yours too.

Shantell Martin is a visual artist, intuitive philosopher, cultural facilitator, teacher, choreographer, songwriter, and performer, and more. She is best known for her line drawings. I appreciate Shantell's consistency, simplicity, and process.

Dacoury Natche (DJ Dahi) is a Grammy-winning record producer, DJ, songwriter, and singer from Inglewood, California. There's a fair chance that at some point, DJ Dahi has been your favorite recording artist's favorite artist. He has driven or contributed to some of my favorite music, including Pusha T and Jay-Z's "Drug Dealers Anonymous," and an album like Childish Gambino's *3.15.20*. He is also known for his work on Kendrick Lamar's album *Good Kid, M.A.A.D City*, Childish Gambino's album *3.15.20*, and for winning a Grammy with 21 Savage on their song,[157] "A Lot."

Vincent Pan (VinnyX) is best known for producing Kodak Black's breakout track "No Flockin," which went on to be certified double platinum and was also the inspiration for Cardi B's smash hit "Bodak Yellow." I was introduced to Vinny through our mutual friend Rob Wang.

Michael Saviello (Big Mike) has been the manager at the iconic East Village barbershop, Astor Place Hairstylists, for nearly 40 years. He paints every day during his lunch break in the back of Astor Place, sometimes with a bottle of wine, sometimes to melodies of jazz. Big Mike's journey is an inspiration and an incredible example of doing things and telling people.

Lindsay Jean Thomson is a writer and community builder. She facilitates #The100DayProject, a free global art project taking place online. I

---

157. https://twitter.com/recordingacad/status/1221563513266532352

would be entirely unsurprised if the next generation's artists emerge from Lindsay's project or other work.

Vin Verma is the founder of Futureland. He makes films, music, and software. I appreciate Vin for his balanced practicality and vision.

About the Author

Herbert Lui is an editorial director and author. He has been writing since he was 15. His work has appeared at publications like Fast Company, Hypebeast, and Quartz, and he later joined Lifehacker as a staff writer. His company Wonder Shuttle has advised organizations such as the City of Toronto, Shopify, and Skillshare on their writing and publications. He writes the Best of Books newsletter, which shares three great books every month.

About Holloway

Holloway publishes books online, offering titles from experts on topics ranging from tools and technology to teamwork and entrepreneurship. All titles are built for a satisfying reading experience on the web as well as in print. The Holloway Reader helps readers find what they need in search results, and permits authors and editors to make ongoing improvements.

Holloway seeks to publish more exceptional authors. We believe that a new company with modern tools can make publishing a better experience for authors and help them reach their audience. If you're a writer with a manuscript or idea, please get in touch at hello@holloway.com.

Made in the USA
Middletown, DE
09 October 2022